OF THE CARMEL OF LISIEUX

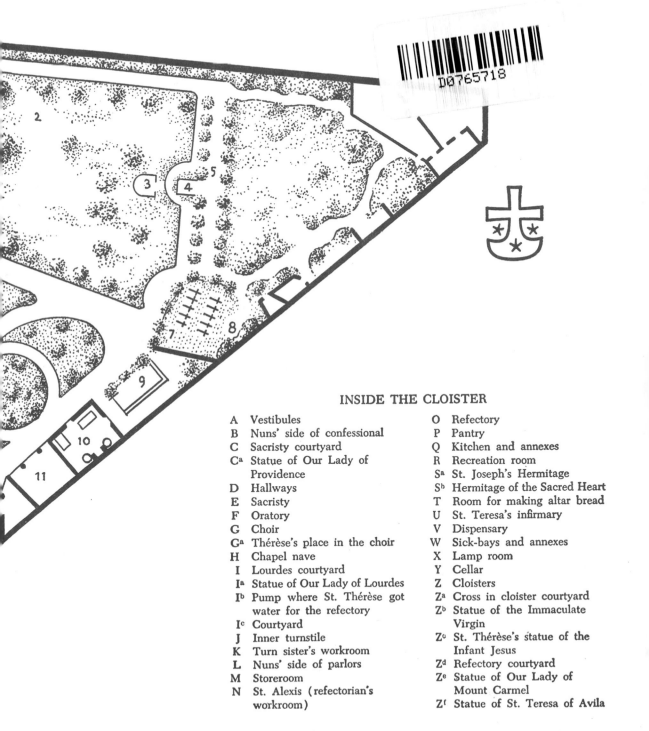

INSIDE THE CLOISTER

A Vestibules
B Nuns' side of confessional
C Sacristy courtyard
Cᵃ Statue of Our Lady of Providence
D Hallways
E Sacristy
F Oratory
G Choir
Gᵃ Thérèse's place in the choir
H Chapel nave
I Lourdes courtyard
Iᵃ Statue of Our Lady of Lourdes
Iᵇ Pump where St. Thérèse got water for the refectory
Iᶜ Courtyard
J Inner turnstile
K Turn sister's workroom
L Nuns' side of parlors
M Storeroom
N St. Alexis (refectorian's workroom)

O Refectory
P Pantry
Q Kitchen and annexes
R Recreation room
Sᵃ St. Joseph's Hermitage
Sᵇ Hermitage of the Sacred Heart
T Room for making altar bread
U St. Teresa's infirmary
V Dispensary
W Sick-bays and annexes
X Lamp room
Y Cellar
Z Cloisters
Zᵃ Cross in cloister courtyard
Zᵇ Statue of the Immaculate Virgin
Zᶜ St. Thérèse's statue of the Infant Jesus
Zᵈ Refectory courtyard
Zᵉ Statue of Our Lady of Mount Carmel
Zᶠ Statue of St. Teresa of Avila

THE PHOTO ALBUM OF
ST. THÉRÈSE OF LISIEUX

February 2, 1993

Dearest Candy,

May you enjoy
this book with my
love -

Happy Birthday

Bunni

THE PHOTO ALBUM OF

st. thérèse

OF LISIEUX

Office Central De Lisieux

Commentary by

François de Sainte-Marie, o.c.d.

Translated by

Peter-Thomas Rohrbach, o.c.d.

CHRISTIAN CLASSICS
Westminster, Maryland
1990

First Published, 1962
Reprinted by Christian Classics, 1990
Second printing by Christian Classics, 1991

This authorized edition has been made from *Le Visage de Thérèse of Lisieux,* 2 vols. Lisieux, Calvados: Office Central de Lisieux

© In the French edition by Office Central de Lisieux, 1961
© In the English translation by P. J. Kenedy & Sons, New York, and Harvill Press, London, 1962

This edition is reprinted by arrangement with Macmillan Publishing Company, a division of Macmillan, Inc.

IMPRIMI POTEST:
CHRISTOPHER LATIMER, O.C.D., *Provincial*
November 30, 1961
NIHIL OBSTAT:
Edward J. Montano, S.T.D., *Censor Librorum*
IMPRIMATUR:
✚ FRANCIS CARDINAL SPELLMAN, *Archbishop of New York*
New York, February 20, 1962

The nihil obstat and imprimatur are official declarations that a book or pamphlet is free of doctrinal or moral error. No implication is contained therein that those who have granted the nihil obstat and imprimatur agree with the contents, opinions or statements expressed.

ISBN 0 87061 177 1

Library of Congress Catalog Card Number: 90 83220

PRINTED AND MANUFACTURED IN THE
UNITED STATES OF AMERICA

CONTENTS

Translator's Preface

St. Thérèse of Lisieux died on the last day of September in 1897, and she was canonized not quite twenty-eight years later. Pope Pius XI called her meteoric rise to fame a "hurricane of glory." And so it was—an astonishing story of miracles, accolades from the Popes, and acclaim from people all over the world.

Caught in the backlash of this hurricane, the nuns at the Carmel of Lisieux found themselves confronted with almost unending requests for information and additional facts about the young Saint who had lived in their convent. After the publication of Thérèse's autobiography, *The Story of A Soul,* in 1898 (just one year from the time of her death!), the nuns subsequently released a volume of statements she made during the last few months of her life, then biographies of her parents, then her letters, and finally, in 1956, the complete and unedited version of her autobiography. Over the years the Carmel also issued a steady stream of pictures: first, some original or only slightly retouched photographs, then some heavily re-touched photographs which made the Saint almost unrecognizable beneath layers of water colors, and finally the paintings and charcoal drawings, composed chiefly by her sister Céline, which presented a rosy-cheeked, rather vacant-looking Thérèse.

The present album is the last significant piece of historical data to be released by the Carmel to the general public. It represents the entire dossier of actual photographs of the Saint in the possession of the Carmel. The photographs are presented in a spirit of historical objectivity, something which is especially useful in light of the charges which have been made against the Carmel in the past few decades. The charges—that there were fraud and some amount of deceit in presenting Thérèse to the Catholic world—are both unfortunate and unfounded. I have written about this elsewhere, and I sincerely hope we have laid this ghost to rest once and for all.

Father François, in his careful and scholarly introduction, gives the reason for the retouching done on the photographs and the spirit behind the idealized portraits issued by the Carmel. His discussion, valuable as it is for an understanding of the pictures of St. Thérèse, is also a commentary on the history of religious art in modern times. With him, we can deplore the artistic values of the Lisieux Carmel, but his comments offer an insight into the artistic mentality of the era.

The photographs themselves present an unusual opportunity to view the face and features of a canonized saint. For those who are well acquainted with St. Thérèse and her life, the photographs have much to contribute to our further understanding of her. For example, in photograph 36, a group picture in which the nuns seem to have assembled without too much regard for order of seniority, we can see Thérèse standing immediately next to Sister Thérèse of St. Augustine, the nun for whom she felt a natural antipathy, as she described it in the *Autobiography*. Or again, we can notice in many photographs that Thérèse's extra black veil, which the nuns donned just for the pose, is slightly askew and hurriedly arranged. We know from other testimony that Thérèse was a neat and fastidious person, but it seems she approached the photographs with an air of indifference and almost impatience. These are some of the small things that give us an added insight.

But the photographs have much to tell people who have little previous acquaintance with St. Thérèse. As Father François notes, we can see a saint come alive again in her milieu. And through the succession of photographs, we can witness Thérèse growing weaker and more feeble as tuberculosis ravishes her body and grim temptations against faith assail her soul. Her face becomes more drawn and tragic in the pictures immediately preceding her death. And then, in the astonishing 46th picture, taken the day after her death, Thérèse's face is bright and tranquil again like a child's, and a slight smile plays around her lips. The storm is over, and we can almost see the heavenly Thérèse.

In fairness to the Carmelite nuns, we might note that the photographs do appear to corroborate one statement they have been making over the years—that, because of the primitive photographic equipment employed, and Thérèse's own particularly mobile features, she did not take an exceptionally good photograph. Thérèse's face takes on a different cast throughout the photographs of the album, and at times it is difficult to realize it is the same person. A graphic proof of this can be noted in the pictures taken just a few minutes apart: photographs 37 and 38, for example, which were taken in July 1896, and photographs 41, 42, and 43 taken on June 7, 1897.

The photographs underscore once again a fundamental theme of St. Thérèse's message for us: the simple, uneventful fabric of her life. Pope Pius XI said she became a saint "without going beyond the common order of things." There is nothing of the spectacular, nothing of the dramatic in her short twenty-four years of life. She is a saint of the ordinary, and she shows us how to be a saint in the ordinary situations in which we are all involved. The photographs, accordingly, show Thérèse in simple, ordinary situations. With the possible exception of the pictures in which Thérèse is costumed as St. Joan of Arc, there is nothing spectacular or surprising about the setting of these photographs. Most of them are contrived and somewhat artificial groupings of the nuns. But we do have the unique privilege of watching a saint in the setting in which she achieved sanctity.

Father François de Sainte-Marie, O.C.D., the editor of this volume and the author of the introductory notes and commentary, had already distinguished himself as a Theresian scholar by his monumental three-volume edition of the *Autobiography* in 1956. I visited him at our monastery in Paris in the summer of 1959, and we discussed the publication of this album which he was working on at that time. We had further discussions about it when he visited me here at the Washington monastery in 1960. He suggested that this translation should adapt his original notes to the mentality of an English-speaking audience. Accordingly, I have omitted a few small things here and there throughout the text which would be of value or interest only to a French audience, and I have added a few phrases of explanation whenever I felt Fr. François was commenting on something that might not be too well known to readers outside of France. Furthermore, I have added some sentences to the captions indicating St. Thérèse's age and phase of life at the time the picture was taken.

On August 30, 1961, some six months after the publication of the French edition of this album, Father François met an untimely and accidental death. He was a wise and careful scholar; and a fine gentleman, too, gentle, kind and friendly. His passing is an irreplaceable loss for the Discalced Carmelite Order. We shall all miss him very much.

(Very Rev.) PETER-THOMAS ROHRBACH, O.C.D.

Washington, D.C.
November 28, 1961

Commentator's Preface

WE OWE A DEBT OF GRATITUDE to the Carmel of Lisieux for the publication of this album. All of the photographs come from its archives. The great majority of them were never published before, and the nuns who had charge of them were generous enough to discuss them with me at great length and answer all my questions patiently. And the appetite of a research worker is an insatiable one!

This volume is a companion piece to *The Autobiography of St. Thérèse of Lisieux,* the unedited manuscript released in 1956. We are now able to view the authentic text of the autobiography, but we should also be able to view the authentic face which bent over it and is still reflected in it. Employing the same kind of objective research we used in publishing the autobiography, we now present St. Thérèse's face to the public through the medium of unretouched photographs.

There is one question, however, which the present volume is forced to discuss in a rather incomplete and inadequate way. Thérèse's sister Céline (in religion Sister Geneviève of the Holy Face) is scarcely mentioned here except in her role as an artist, and her artistic work has been the subject of intense controversy. The impartial reader can gain a broader perspective of her life and make a more accurate judgment by reading *A Memoir of My Sister, St. Thérèse,* in which Céline unconsciously describes herself with her engaging and impulsive character, her gifts, her admitted faults, and her touching faith.

Furthermore, I must state that I alone am responsible for the opinions expressed in these pages, although the Carmel, with great fairness, has authorized me to express them.

Finally, I must mention Sister Marie-Emmanuel of St. Joseph, who offered so much assistance in the matter of the preparation for publication of St. Thérèse's *Autobiography* and in the preparation of this volume. During the course of this work which she undertook so enthusiastically, she departed for a world where historical problems do not exist because history is viewed there in the Eternal Presence.

J. François de Sainte-Marie
o. c. d.

I.
Photography in a Carmelite Convent

A PHOTOGRAPH ALBUM of a saint who was also a cloistered nun could cause some justifiable surprise. These pictures were taken when there was no idea there would ever be such intense interest in the face of Sister Thérèse of the Infant Jesus. And now, upon the release of the photographs, it might seem that these nuns who had veiled their faces to lay people rather liked to pose before the camera.

The saints of history, in their humility, were extremely reluctant to pose for a painting or drawing, and it demanded some enterprise on the part of a painter to sketch even a hurried likeness. A painter needed a certain amount of cleverness to obtain any kind of result with a saint. St. Laurence of Brindisi was painted while he was preaching a sermon, and St. Francis Regis while celebrating Mass. The painter, Simon François, studied St. Vincent de Paul for an entire year during mealtime or in the church to get material for his portrait. And sometimes even saints devised ruses for artists to obtain portraits of other saints. For example, the painter Giuseppe de Cesari, using a plan outlined for him by St. Philip Neri, forced St. Felix of Cantilice to wait for an alms he was seeking and took advantage of the time to sketch his portrait. The saintly prioress of the Carmelites of Granada chose the moment when St. John of the Cross fell into an ecstasy to call in an artist to paint him, although the final result seems to have been a disappointment.

On the other hand, St. Catharine of Bologna, that cultured saint who composed Latin hymns, painted, and wrote music, has left us her own self-portrait, which now hangs in the Gallery of Art in Venice. And St. Teresa of Avila consented to pose for a painting, trying to sit "without budging her head or her eyes" and holding her hands joined at shoulder height—however, the painting itself, by Brother Juan de la Miseria, a former student of Sanchez Coello, is a poor one.

But on the whole, the saints refused to pose for posterity. When St. Francis Borgia was in his death agony, he still had enough perception to observe an artist sketching his portrait as he crouched behind one of the priests. St. Francis gestured him away so violently that the bystanders had to comply with the dying man's request and send the artist away, as we know from the testimony of his own brother at the saint's Process of Canonization.

And although the invention of photography eliminated the problems of sitting and posing for a painting, most of the saints of the last century still refused to have their pictures taken. Even a cursory examination of Schamoni's excellent book, *The Face of the Saints*, will demonstrate the few pictures we possess of saints who lived during the second half of the nineteenth century and died before Thérèse of Lisieux. Only St. Bernadette seems to have allowed herself to be photographed willingly, if we can judge by the number of surviving photographs. She went to the photographer's at Lourdes when a demand grew for her picture. However, she declared emphatically: "If the photographer does not think me beautiful enough, I will not add a single pin to make myself look prettier." But she did pose, kneeling with her rosary in hand, in the same posture she had during the apparitions, or else before a little altar. There is a certain simplicity in these poses, something of the kind we see in the photographs of St. Thérèse. Several pictures were taken of St. Bernadette later at Nevers, and there is one official photograph made at the request of the Bishop of Tarbes, who was trying to suppress a fictitious picture then being circulated for the price of two *sous*.

But this does not solve our problem here, since we are discussing cloistered nuns unknown at the time to the general public.

The first bit of evidence we receive, though, is reassuring. St. Thérèse was photographed on only one occasion during her first six years in the convent, and the two pictures taken at that time in January 1889, were due to rather accidental circumstances. The Abbé Gombault, with the permission of the Bishop of Bayeux, had entered the cloister to give the nuns instructions on the use of gas light which was being installed. The priest took two pictures of Thérèse, then a novice, in order to give them to her father and sister. These were the first pictures ever taken inside the Carmel of Lisieux.

In 1894, soon after the death of her father, Céline joined the Carmel and was reunited with her older sisters, Marie and Pauline, and with Thérèse, her younger sister, who had been her childhood playmate and confidante. Before she entered the convent, Céline had become interested in art, and both she and her cousin, Marie Guérin, had acquired a deep enthusiasm for photography. The art of photography was no longer in its epic period, nor even in the grand period of Napoleon III, but as a manual of the time states, ". . . it has become a modish distraction."

Céline brought her photographic equipment with her to the Carmel, a 13/18 Darlot, with all of the necessary accessories. The original Carmelite legislation of St. Teresa had certainly not contemplated photographic equipment, but Céline received permission for it from Mother Agnes of Jesus, who had been prioress since 1893. It aroused considerable interest on the part of the nuns, most of whom had never seen a camera before. It was inevitable, then, that the young photographer be asked to take a picture on some community feast, or on a profession day, or even when the nuns were all gathered for some common task. The iconography of the convent, rather meager until that point, became considerably enriched. Forty-one pictures, in which St. Thérèse appears either alone or in a group, are extant from the years 1894 to 1897. This large quantity of photographs could cause surprise only if one were unacquainted with the family atmosphere existing in most Carmels, where each nun attempts, according to the charming phrase of St. Teresa of Avila, to put the little talent and wit she has received from God at the service of her sisters.

Doubtlessly, Céline's equipment would not have been allowed in every Carmelite convent. We ourselves know of one convent where a nun, a venerable jubilarian, was photographed in complete secrecy so as to avoid any possible scandal. But the Carmel at Lisieux, like many of the convents of that time, was a strange combination of austerity and freedom. St. Thérèse's correspondence shows how eagerly the nuns accepted the little delicacies presented by her father, while at the same time the convent was kept unbearably cold. Today things are much more carefully regulated, but at that time the prioress possessed an unlimited amount of authority.

The nuns also made use of the photographs in their correspondence with other convents of the Order. The nuns at Poitiers, the convent from which Lisieux had been founded, as well as those at Dijon and at Tours, expressed great interest in the four Martin sisters, particularly in Thérèse, about whom Mother Marie de Gonzague had written such glowing accounts. The nuns felt they could give a better description by sending a citrate contact-proof of one of the photographs, rather than attempt an awkward written description, as St. Teresa of Avila had to do when she was describing the mouth of her novice, Sister Isabella.

On the back of a photograph—since unfortunately lost—sent to the Carmel of Tours in 1893, Mother Marie de Gonzague wrote about St. Thérèse, who was then twenty:

The jewel of Carmel, its dear Benjamin. She has the office of painter, in which she excels without having had any lessons other than observing our Reverend Mother, her sister, at work. Mature and strong, with the air of a child, and with a sound of voice and manner of expression which veils the wisdom and perfection of a woman fifty years old. A soul which is always calm and in complete possession of herself at all times. A completely innocent saint, who needs no repentance to appear before God, but whose head is always full of mischief. Mystic, comic, she can make you weep with devotion, and just as easily die with laughter at recreation.

Sometimes there was an exchange of negatives with the families of the nuns. After Abbé Gombault took the two photographs of St. Thérèse for her father, he was sent to the Martin home, Les Buissonnets, to photograph M. Martin and Léonie. Thérèse makes allusion to these photographs in her correspondence with Céline and with her cousin Mme. La Néele. The nuns were forbidden to keep photographs, even those of their parents, but during recreation they were allowed to look at the community's photograph album in which all the Carmel's photographs were kept and which was later used, with Céline's help, to identify the nuns in the pictures.

Some photographic manuals of the period, that era which was so oppressively concerned with pose and décor, give us an indication of the principles Céline employed in taking her pictures. Klary's *Guide de l'Amateur Photographe* (Paris, 1888) advises: "Have the model pose in some characteristic situation or occupation. A soldier, for example, could lean on his rifle, a fisherman could hold a line in his hand. The best results will be obtained by photographing the model as if he were doing something. The model may read, play an instrument, examine some objects." And the photographs were posed against those artificial painted backdrops: The parlor with the small table and the inevitable Gothic armchair, the garden with its romantic old trees and white statue, the seaport, the monastery— and, of course, the wooden column with the Corinthian capital which could be raised or lowered according to the height of the client.

Céline, therefore, arranged and posed the groups for her photographs in accordance with the artistic mood of the period. For her backgrounds, she employed all the possibilities the convent had to offer: The cloister, the outdoor crucifix, the statues in the courts and gardens. Everything a Carmelite nun could use figures in her pictures—the hourglass, the freshly cut lily, the rosary, holy pictures exhibited like signposts, the staff from the statue of the Good Shepherd, sacred vessels and other accessories from the sacristy. She even employed the amateur costume that was made for Thérèse when she took the role of St. Joan of Arc during a religious play in the convent: The wig, the cardboard sword, the paper lilies, the helmet, the chain, the traditional prisoner's pitcher of water; and a cross, laid carefully on the ground, completing the scene.

While Céline arranged the groups for the photographs and focused the camera, it was usually some other nun who took the actual picture. Sister St. John of the Cross frequently served as the operator.

Although Céline showed real talent in the arrangement of her photographs, she did not know how to avoid fixed expressions and stereotyped gestures. Certain poses of Thérèse kneeling are a little theatrical. But on the other hand, some photographs of the nuns taken without any posing and in a natural setting—during recreation among the trees, the washing, the haying—are completely successful. And if the expression on the faces in some of these photographs is wooden and fixed, the fault is not necessarily Céline's. The cameras of the period did not admit enough light, nor were the plates sufficiently sensitive, and some poses had to be held for nine seconds of exposure time. It was quite difficult to retain one's naturalness during all that time. This was a vexing problem to the photographers of that period because their art could only be used to immobilize flowers, animals, and people, while the impressionistic painters were able to capture an instant mood on their canvases. "The changes of expression are so quick and the nuances so fleeing," writes Liébert, an eighteenth-century photographer, "that one would want to capture them immediately on a sensitive plate. You have to reanimate and revive this expression continually throughout the duration of the pose, and this presents great difficulties. You must talk to the model during the pose and attempt to arouse the expression you want to see in the photograph, if it is to be successful."

The problem of attempting to capture the attention of a whole group of nuns was even more difficult. After a few seconds, some of the faces grew tense, their smiles forced, their bodies stiff, and weariness settled over the group. Thérèse, whose features, as we will discuss, were particularly mobile, was least able to sustain a long pose. In many of the photographs her face is blurred because she moved, her lips pinched, and her smile no longer natural. It is well to remember, at the outset, these limitations of the photographs so that we do not demand too much of them.

II.

A Smiling and Expressive Face

As we view the face of St. Thérèse through the medium of the primitive photography of the nineteenth century, we should take into account the testimony of her contemporaries to help us evaluate the photographs. But we must note that the statements of her own sisters in the Process of Beatification are unfortunately not always completely impartial, because of the admiration and affection they bore for their sister. Céline certainly had seen children as pretty as her sister, but she claims that Thérèse possessed "something which I have never seen in other children, that combination of the supernatural and the natural which gave her a unique and exquisite charm."

The saint's three sisters all give the same testimony in the Process about Thérèse's angelic expression, and the other nuns of the Carmel seem to have shared their opinion. "The first time I saw Sister Thérèse of the Infant Jesus," recalls Sister Marthe of Jesus, "she gave me the impression of an angel. Her face had a truly heavenly radiance, and this impression endured, not only during her postulancy, but throughout her whole religious life." Another nun exclaimed at recreation: "Look at Sister Thérèse. Wouldn't you say she comes from heaven? She looks like an angel." Mother Marie of the Angels, who reported this incident, further notes that "along with her composed manner she combined the charming attitude of a child which gave her a candor and innocence."

A visiting nun from another community who met Thérèse in the parlor said she was captivated by the young nun. She said: "How charming that child is! She appears to be more of heaven than of earth. There is something so pure and so honest about her that just seeing her makes you feel peaceful." Lay people who visited the convent said there was "something heaven-like in her eyes." Louise Delarue, who had received First Communion with Thérèse, could not forget her "air of innocence and extraordinary candor" and stressed the last word particularly.

This variety of testimonies must indicate an important fact: Thérèse Martin assuredly possessed a unique charm in which her smile figured largely, that smile which seems a little stiff in the photographs and which the colored prints have further disfigured. Her real smile was not born of good manners nor a natural optimism. While she possessed a good disposition and even liked to indulge in some mischief, the real source of her smile must be attributed to an entirely different cause. Thérèse stated, as reported by Mother Marie of the Angels: "When I am suffering a lot, instead of looking sad I react with a smile. At first I wasn't always successful, but now it is a habit I've happily acquired." Thus, St. Thérèse's engaging smile emanates from the depths of physical and spiritual suffering borne with astonishing interior strength.

I was able to interrogate one of St. Thérèse's last contemporaries, M. Rixe, a notary-public. While on his way to work each morning, he met the young girl returning from Mass with her father. M. Rixe stated: "I just stopped and stared at her, that little girl with her mass of golden hair." Another contemporary, Canon Jomard, Vicar General of the diocese of Rouen, reports the testimony given to him by two of her former teachers at the Benedictine Abbey school, Mother St. Léon and Mother Stanislas: "She wasn't exactly pretty; her chin was a little large, but she had marvelous blonde hair and a touching air of innocence."

Even more valuable is the testimony of a pharmacist from Lisieux, M. Lahaye, who was present at the Carmel during Thérèse's profession ceremony and who had an excellent opportunity to study her face. His description is rather flowery, and it might make us fear he has been guilty of some idealization, but he does indicate Thérèse's principal traits. He states: "During her profession ceremony, I was standing in the sanctuary and could see her behind the grill. The black veil she was going to receive was covered with a crown of roses and lying on the altar. The white veil she was still wearing had been raised and I could see the fine symmetry of her features. Nevertheless, her forehead was slightly convex, the nose short, the mouth almost large, the chin quite large and rounded, and although her cheeks were not hollow, her cheek-bones were a little prominent. Her eyes possessed a brilliance that was tempered by candor and purity, but on that moving occasion their natural gentleness was supplanted by a certain gravity. Her color was like new ivory, transparent with a hint of amber and rose color. She seemed slender despite her heavy religious habit."

This description seems authentic, because we can recognize in it the undeniable features of the Martin family, particularly the chin.

The first official description of St. Thérèse issued by the Carmel in the 1907 edition of *The Story of a Soul* does not seem quite as authentic; it sounds more like an awkward description of Ribera's portrait of St. Teresa of Avila. The 1915 description is an idealized one which contains some accurate details, but it eradicates the individuality of her features in a burst of sentimentality: "She was tall. She had blonde hair, deep blue eyes, delicate eyebrows, tiny mouth, and delicate and even features. Her face was lily-white and in perfect proportion, and always had a serenity and heavenly peace about it. Finally, her bearing was full of dignity, but at the same time simple and graceful."

Perhaps Fernand Laudet gave us the best description in a book on St. Thérèse published in 1927: "Some assure us that she was very beautiful, others that her face was charming, but I believe it would be more accurate to say that her face was a little irregular, although it did possess a charm. She had two large blue eyes, under very straight eyebrows, and her complexion was lily-like and surmounted by a cloud of golden hair. People said: 'She has a heavenly look.' "

III.

The Limitations of a Photograph

THE TESTIMONY of our witnesses about the charm of St. Thérèse's face helps us to understand the attitude of the Martin sisters and the Lisieux Carmel regarding the Saint's photographs. They were disappointed in not finding in the pictures that indefinable charm which they remembered in Thérèse, and they immediately scratched the word "defective" across the gelatine plate of certain pictures. They wanted to destroy these pictures, and it is only thanks to Céline's prudence that they did not succeed. Due to her foresight, we were able to recover these photographs, sometimes pressed between the pages of a book, sometimes hidden in an envelope. But, despite all this, Céline still shared her sisters' misgivings about the value of a photograph as a valid historical document.

Her attitude expressed the general feeling prevalent in artistic circles after the first half of the last century. Baudelaire's depreciating statement is well known: "A new industry has arisen which has contributed no little to perpetuating the sheer stupidity of the belief that art is only the faithful reproduction of nature. This industry, invading art, has become its mortal enemy." Baudelaire, of course, was ultimately to change his opinion, as did the greater part of the intellectuals of the time. Lamartine, who had been among the first to oppose the new invention, at first said, "It is nothing more than a ray of sunlight flashed on a model," but later stated, "We no longer say it is a trade, it is an art, even more than an art, a phenomenon of light in which the artist collaborates with the sun." In December 1862, the outstanding artists of the Institute signed a harsh statement which reads: "The undersigned artists all protest any attempt to identify photography with art." This statement was heartily approved by those artists of the period who circulated the aphorism: Photography is to painting what a barrel-organ is to music.

However, in February of 1895, the same year in which Céline took the greater part of the pictures in this album, photography began to achieve recognition in the Academies. At Marseilles, Léon Vidal, the esteemed research scholar, wrote enthusiastically: "It is one of the most astonishing scientific conquests of man over nature, done in silence and darkness with the aid of a somewhat mysterious mechanism." Msgr. Ricard, who introduced Vidal to the Marseilles Academy of Sciences, is a little more reserved in his approbation: ". . . that which many call an art, that which is one of the most amazing scientific achievements of our era which produces so many marvels . . ."

Céline, isolated in her cloister from this reappraisal of artistic values, was unaware of the new artistic viewpoint. While she was working in her darkroom—with adroitness, and with love, too—she never considered that she was producing a human document of any value. A close friend and advisor of the Lisieux Carmel, Canon Dubosq, who later became the Promotor of the Faith during the Process of Beatification of St. Thérèse, and who was himself an amateur photographer, wrote to Céline in January of 1911: "Our ideas and our tastes are in absolute agreement regarding the photographic question. There are many who say that photography, because it acts mechanically, is a witness to pure truth, while the work of the artist must be suspected of fantasy and caprice because of the artist's own activity. Well, I believe just the opposite. Very often it is the photograph which is false, while the artist, if he be sensitive and honest, can make his subject live. He can study, feel, observe sentiments and affections, indeed, the very character of his subject; then he gathers these fleeting and most indicative expressions of the face which best reflect the soul of his subject."

Canon Dubosq's reasoning is valid, provided the artist be a great one, because, as Doncœur notes in his preface to Schamoni's *The Face of the Saints*, "It does not seem, in view of the evidence, that physics and chemistry are patient and intelligent enough to contend with genius."

The most renowned artists always seemed to have resisted the use of mechanical processes and technical methods of reproduction. Vincent d'Indy, the musician, was quite hostile to the recording of his "Symphony on a Mountain Air," because he felt the mechanical reproduction of a work of art was blasphemous since it eliminated the presence of the artist himself. Gaston Baty shared the same sentiments when he forbade his interpreters to make use of the new invention, the motion picture.

But let us make clear, in the case of St. Thérèse's photographs, that we do not have a simple choice between a work of art and a mechanical process of reproduction. The choice is between a collection of actual photographs and some paintings of dubious artistic value. Understandably, we must choose the photographs. And so would anyone in this modern era, since we no longer think that a photograph is an inadequate representation of a historical figure.

However, we must try to understand the mentality of Céline who remained unshaken in her conviction that "the eye of the painter is not deceived, especially when it is the eye of a sister." In a final statement, dated February 11, 1950, she furnishes us the key to her artistic work: "I would like to say a word about the *physical portraits* of the Saint. Sheer mechanical processes of reproduction, showing only the plastic structure of her face, cannot capture her soul, any more than they can capture refinement of manners or the perfume of a rose. What I have *always* tried to do is to capture and communicate that indefinable quality which shows the true picture of her soul beneath her features."

IV.
Céline's Paintings

THE QUESTION, then, presents itself: Did Céline possess any real talent for painting?

Her cousin, Jeanne Guérin, felt she did and pleaded with M. Martin to make his daughter study art. That was in January of 1883, when Céline was fourteen. After Céline finished school in 1885, she took lessons under a rather eccentric old lady, Mlle. Godard, a student of Leon Cogniet. It seems that the two never got along well together. "She always tried to suppress my creativity," wrote Céline, who was forced to make some of her paintings without her teacher's knowledge, real "daubs" Céline herself described them. M. Martin was delighted with a painting she did of the Blessed Virgin and St. Mary Magdalene in June of 1888, and offered to send her to Paris for study under qualified experts. She declined because of her vocation to Carmel. Thus, Céline deliberately sacrificed the possibility of artistic development offered to her, because of her religious vocation. When we consider her artistic deficiencies, therefore, we ought to take into account this meritorious sacrifice.

In 1893, M. Guérin, her uncle, introduced her to M. Krug, another student of Cogniet and perhaps of Flandrin, "a fine old man without equal," who had a distinguished reputation for his knowledge of composition and modeling. Krug, who had painted the fresco of the dome of the Abbey at Lisieux, seems to have encouraged Céline and promised he could have her work hung at an exhibition within two years. He gave her a few lessons and left her his large palette as a souvenir. With only this very incomplete training, Céline began to broaden her activities. She received orders for various religious paintings, and in 1892 painted a picture of the Assumption for the main altar of the Hotel-Dieu at Bayeux. She threw herself into this work with all the intensity and all the ingenuity she always employed in whatever she did.

As proof of this, one has only to leaf through the unpublished collection of her work which was assembled in the Carmel at the wish of her sister and prioress, Mother Agnes. This two-volume work, illustrated with numerous photographs, gives a résumé of her artistic accomplishments: painting, drawing, decorating, sculpture, miniatures, and photography. In the prologue, Céline states: "How I should have loved to have been a cook! But even then I would have used all my resources to change and invent and struggle for perfection, since everything interests me. That would almost have become an artistic work for me! I cannot tear myself away from artistic work. I was so fascinated by this kind of work that I even felt I was wasting time when I did any reading other than prayers or the Office."

It is unfortunate that she received so inadequate an artistic formation and that she felt no need to study with real experts. With her lively intelligence and her avid curiosity she would surely have become interested in the history of art, but unfortunately she knew little about it. The Carmel of Lisieux has preserved fifteen albums of various paintings grouped by subjects—Annunciation, Ecce Homo, etc. There are some representations of masterpieces as well as some rather mediocre art work. And the holy pictures used at the Carmel during that period are only cheap reproductions of bad art.

Céline drew her models, if not her inspiration, from these mixed sources. We have many proofs of her eclecticism. For example, she writes about her painting of the Blessed Virgin and St. Mary Magdalene: "This composition should bear the title 'Plagiarism,' since I borrowed the figures from well-known works and simply grouped them to my taste." These "well-known works" are Carlo Dolci's "Mater Dolorosa" and an unsigned picture of Mary Magdalene executed in the ornate taste of the period. The large canvas she painted of the Assumption for a church in Bayeux in 1892 is inspired by Murillo's "Immaculate Conception." Of the Adoration of the Shepherds, painted for the Carmelite choir in 1893, she wrote: "All I did was group figures taken from here and there in the paintings of the masters." The figures in this painting were inspired by Muller's "Adoration of the Shepherds," and the Christ Child by Janssens' "The Flight into Egypt."

When Céline began to sketch a life of St. Thérèse in pictures, she simply borrowed figures from works of different artistic periods and dressed them in the current style. She found her models in widely distributed contemporary prints, in missionary reviews, in periodicals, and on holy cards. I personally examined a large envelope full of cuttings which had been annotated by Céline or Mother Agnes for use in this project. A little girl playing the tambourine from a page in *Winter Evenings* is marked with this note: "Figure of Thérèse looking at her father." Other pictures are to be used "for the length of the arm," "for a neck executed very nicely," "for the proportion of children's heads." Fashion pictures can be used "for Thérèse's jacket when she was fifteen years old," "for her hat in the picture when she is gazing at the stars," "for M. Martin's overcoat." The sleeves of a dress in an advertisement from a store are encircled, "but make sure they reach below the elbow." These give us an indication of why Céline's paintings of Thérèse are so artificial and poorly drawn.

Probably from time to time Canon Dubosq raised his voice to recall in a somewhat neutral way the rules of perspective or anatomy. On April 15, 1921, he wrote her: "I have examined your 'Crucifixion' carefully. The over-all effect is good and one is moved by it. Even the anatomy, despite your insufficient training, is good in general. However, in this respect I might point out a few slight retouches that could profitably be made: 1) the lower shape of the outer large pectoral muscle; 2) from the perspective of the wood of the cross, the eye falls a little too far below Christ's face and too much to the left—thus you show perhaps a bit too much of the top of the head; 3) some of the brush strokes seem to indicate an incorrect contour of the muscular formation or bone structure, for instance, the projecture of the tibia (left leg) is too much slanted toward the outside. The same is true of certain contours particularly around the kneecap and the inner forward muscle to the right (on the left thigh). But all this *is not important*."

Canon Dubosq's advice was not always heeded, perhaps because of the technical nature of his language.

Céline notes in her *Memoir* that she painted two pictures of Thérèse at Les Buissonnets between 1885 and 1888: one, a half-length portrait of Thérèse; the other, Thérèse seated in a meadow surrounded by flowers. These apparently did not satisfy her, for she eventually painted other pictures over them. In the convent, she never painted her sister during her lifetime. However, during Thérèse's final illness, when Mother Agnes was preparing herself to be the custodian and editor of the autobiography, Céline began to make plans for the paintings she would do in the future. She writes: "During her final illness when I began to foresee what I would

have to do, I made her pose for me, and I studied her features carefully so that I would not forget them. And her expression became engraved in my heart."

The Story of a Soul was originally published without any of Céline's drawings. The Carmel deserves praise for its sober use of illustrations in that first edition of 1898. There are only two illustrations: an actual, unretouched photograph of Thérèse holding her rosary, which was used as a frontispiece; and a photograph of the convent and of Thérèse's cell, which was placed in the middle of the volume. But some friends of the Carmel who affected a knowledge of these matters persuaded the nuns that the frontispiece of a biography ought to be a half-length portrait of the book's subject. "We decided," Céline wrote, "to paint such a portrait which would be a composite of all the photographs we possessed of our Saint."

This portrait was based principally on an 1894 photograph of a group of nuns in the Lourdes grotto, which shows Thérèse with her hands joined. "But I had to do this portrait over many times, because I was unsuccessful at first. Thérèse had moved in the picture, and I had to consult other photographs to capture her resemblance." The result was the oval charcoal portrait of St. Thérèse which was used as the frontispiece after 1889. It was modified a number of times, principally after the beatification in 1923 when a glow was painted around her head, and after the canonization when the halo of the saints was added.

Msgr. de Teil, who was the Vice-Postulator of the cause and prepared the Process of Beatification of Sister Thérèse of the Infant Jesus, made a request in 1911 for a three-color portrait to be used as a frontispiece to the Articles in the Cause. Again it was a question of an oval portrait. This distinguished and prudent prelate, who described himself as caught "between the anvil and the hammer, between the requirements of Rome and the reserved nature of the Normans," expressed great admiration for the portrait Céline had executed at his request, although he was disturbed about the heavy red lips. "You would think that Sister Thérèse painted her lips," he wrote.

His admiration was shared by the members of the Diocesan Tribunal, and the oval portrait was hung in the room where they conducted their sessions. In her correspondence, Céline writes about an official approbation for this portrait, but there is no mention of it in the Acts of the Process. However, the Promotor of the Faith, Canon Dubosq, who was the principal figure at the tribunal, wrote in a letter of April 30, 1911: "The only enduring portrait is the one used as the frontispiece to *The Story of a Soul*. It speaks to the soul, and one would like to see it used always." He advised the Car-

Oval half-length portrait of Thérèse made in charcoal by Sister Geneviève of the Holy Face, in one of its earlier renditions

mel to make the following statement about the portrait: "This half-length portrait has been composed from photographs and from long and daily observation of the living model. The people who lived with Sister Thérèse all testify that it is a faithful representation of her as she appeared at the age of twenty-two."

The interrogation at the Cause for Beatification seemed to pass rather quickly over the question of the portraits, as it did over the question of the autobiography, since these appeared to be secondary matters at that time. During the Ordinary Process, Mother Agnes was asked if she knew how the portraits in *The Story of a Soul* were prepared, and she answered: "Most of these portraits are paintings done by our sister, Céline, from family recollections and from some photographs we possessed. We had a camera at Carmel which Céline knew how to operate very well. She used it in connection with certain drawings she was making and several times photographed Sister Thérèse and other members of the community. To please us, the Servant of God submitted to all our requests for pictures with complete simplicity."

The Cause for Beatification progressed with amazing speed, and after 1910 Msgr. de Teil asked the Carmel to do a full portrait of Thérèse "which would correctly depict her character and indicate her own particular kind of spirituality for the devotion of the faithful." The 1912 drawing of Thérèse scattering roses on her crucifix was the answer to this request. Céline used an 1895 photograph of Thérèse in the St. Joan of Arc costume as a model for the face, but she was dismayed when, in attempting to rectify the mistakes of her first portrait, she made the new mistake of drawing the eyes too large. Msgr. de Teil, however, declared he was enchanted: "All my compliments to Sister Geneviève for the realistic expression on the face, and for the wonderful effect given by the hands lovingly pressing the crucifix." He did, though, adopt the criticism of Canon Dubosq about the proportion of the hands, and he asked that the chin be made a little stronger.

This drawing of Thérèse with the roses appeared for the first time in the 1914 edition of *The Story of a Soul*. In 1925, Céline did another version of the same subject, this time in color, and she attempted to correct the faults of the first drawing. She was completely satisfied with the result: "I put all my heart into it. After I had completed it, I was looking at it one day and it seemed so realistic and so alive that I could not restrain my tears. It seemed that my Thérèse was actually looking at me. In my opinion, it is the best resemblance of her." This portrait was reproduced in sepia in *The Story of a Soul* after 1925, and was widely disseminated in color pictures and postcards. A note in the 1925 edition, which followed the "Introduction

Thérèse with roses. Painted by Sister Geneviève of the Holy Face

to the Portraits," maintained that this was the manner in which Thérèse often appeared in the various reported visions of her.

The oval portrait, and the one of Thérèse holding the roses, are just two of the many paintings done by Céline. All of these paintings were used, at one time or another, to illustrate different editions of *The Story of a Soul,* and they have been collected in *Vie en Images de Sainte Thérèse de l'Enfant-Jésus,* published by the Central Office in Lisieux.

In the years after 1915, Céline donated her time exclusively to artistic work at the request of her prioress, Mother Agnes. And both of them commissioned other artists to execute paintings, among them Jouvenot, who did the washes for the albums *Vie en Images, La Petite Voie,* and *Les Miracles de Ste. Thérèse de l'Enfant-Jésus.*

There was much to keep the two sisters busy: the progress of the Cause, contacts with outsiders, and numerous arrangements to be made at Lisieux and at the birthplace of Thérèse in Alençon. They were not professional artists, trying to develop their own talents, but cloistered nuns involved in an extraordinary spiritual adventure, attempting to use all their good will and every means at hand to cope with the amazing popularity of their sister, this "child loved by the whole world."

V.

The Retouched Photographs

The photographs of St. Thérèse, at least those destined for publication, were retouched according to the same principles Céline had used in her paintings and charcoal drawings. She did the retouching with water colors, pencil, and charcoal on special enlargements which fortunately left the original negatives intact.

Sur l'authenticité des Portraits de Sainte Thérèse de l'Enfant-Jésus, a brochure published by Lisieux in 1949, presents an example of Céline's retouching as it discusses the photograph of Thérèse kneeling in the garden taken on June 7, 1897. "Following Canon Dubosq's advice, Céline used the third pose taken that day, the clearest and the one in which the clothing falls in the best arrangement, and tried to incorporate the sweet and virtuous smile from the second pose."

In addition, the photographs were sometimes remounted on other photographs. Thus, the celebrated photograph of Thérèse meditating in the cemetery was achieved by cutting her figure from a group picture of the community, retouching the face, and then mounting it on a picture of the convent garden and cemetery.

Some of the retouched photographs were used, along with Céline's paintings, to illustrate different editions of *The Story of a Soul.* The 1902 edition contained photographs of Thérèse as a novice in a white mantle, Thérèse meditating in the garden and cemetery, and a view of her corpse

THE RETOUCHED PHOTOGRAPHS

laid out in the choir. This latter picture was eliminated in following editions, but the other two were retained. In 1923, another retouched photograph was added: Thérèse as a novice without her white mantle. The two photographs of Thérèse as a novice were the ones taken by Abbé Gombault, and their repeated use is explained by the fact that they had been circulated secretly and were provoking much discussion.

Two other photographs were added in the 1933 edition: Thérèse kneeling in the garden, which was the retouched third pose of the June 7, 1897, picture; and a picture of Thérèse during her final illness, in which a black veil had been painted over her white woolen cap. These five photographs were used as illustrations between 1940 and 1946. Because of a lack of paper and printing difficulties, no photographs appeared in the editions after the war from 1947 to 1950. However, in the second French edition of Abbé Combes' conclusive *Spirituality of St. Thérèse* three photographs were published, all of them unretouched: Thérèse at eight years of age, Thérèse at fifteen, and Thérèse holding the pictures of the Infant Jesus and of the Holy Face.

In the 1953 and 1955 French editions of *The Story of a Soul* the following photographs were used, all of them containing some degree of retouching: an enlargement from the June 7, 1897, half-length photograph; Thérèse at recreation with the community among the chestnut trees; the Gombault novice photograph; and Thérèse as sacristan. There was also included the interesting photograph of Thérèse doing the community wash, which appeared without any retouching. The facsimile edition of the autobiography, issued in 1956, contained the magnificent and exactly reproduced July 1896 photograph of Thérèse holding a lily.

Furthermore, Céline fearlessly corrected some of the paintings of artists commissioned by the Carmel. The only picture fully acceptable to the Martin sisters was the Roybet portrait donated to the Carmel in 1917 by Baroness Gérard, and even this painting had to be corrected by the artist in accordance with the nuns' request. Roybet was a celebrated artist of the time, famous for his portrait of General Galliéni, and Marie wrote about his painting of Thérèse: "Everyone thinks it is an artistic marvel. I find that it expresses the truth."

Sometimes Céline was so carried away by her enthusiasm that not much of the original artist's work remained. She writes about the painting of Thérèse gazing at the stars: "I was assisted by an artist from Paris. When he had completed his work, I refashioned Thérèse's profile and gave Papa another head. I did the head over completely, and turned him around the other way. I had a difficult time of it, but now we are completely satisfied."

Painting by Ferdinand Roybet

In January, 1929, she announced to Léonie that practically nothing remained of an Italian portrait which she did over completely.

Céline obeyed a consuming hunger for perfection, as did Mother Agnes in another area, and this quest compelled her to make endless corrections on paintings which dissatisfied her since her abilities were not equal to her ideals. This is a family character trait which explains for us the continual retouching done by the Martin sisters on the paintings and photographs in their possession. They were disappointed at not finding that indefinable quality which fascinated them about Thérèse, and they carefully tried to reconstruct it by incessant, but questionable, retouchings.

They followed a current norm of beauty, more prevalent in religious art than in the art of the academies, which led them to identify the beautiful with the pretty and graceful. In speaking of Thérèse's affected pose in the photographs where she was costumed as St. Joan of Arc, Céline said: "In that picture you can see the effect we like." And when Céline retouched her own picture taken in a group with Thérèse at the foot of the cross on the day of her profession, she made her own face a perfect oval. This was the innocent affectation practiced by all the photographers of that period when the object was to make a person look as nice as possible. But was it so innocent? Not quite so innocent, since it changed a person's face, and consequently, the impression of his character. It is no more legitimate to modify a person's face than his temperament or his character.

Many people in the last century felt that a work of art had to be an idealization of reality. Céline simply belonged to her time when she gave this indicative advice to the painter Roybet: "I believe you will satisfy us, sir, if you paint Thérèse with a heavenly expression; if you manage to make her an ideal and beautiful person. You know her well enough now not to depart from this type. And that will be sufficient."

Pauline, Marie, and Céline all shared the same artistic belief. St. Thérèse herself has written that she admired and cherished the literary and artistic accomplishments of her sisters. Their idealism was particularly regrettable because it was in sharp opposition to their own healthy realism which so splendidly equipped them for practical affairs and business matters. Only Léonie, at the Visitation convent in Caen, seemed not completely in sympathy with her sisters in this regard, if one can judge from some correspondence addressed to her by her sisters. Marie wrote to her on July 16, 1913: "Do not complain that Céline has idealized our Saint. In none of her portraits do I see her as beautiful as she was in reality."

However, let us repeat that the Martin sisters were simply conforming to the ideas of their time. The correspondence of Canon Dubosq with

Céline gives evidence of this feeling: "A violent and indiscreet and brutal realism only weakens the expression, instead of strengthening it. I am aware that certain Spanish and Flemish artists feel quite differently about it, but the Italian and the French believe more in the use of a discreet idealism than in a brutal and excessively natural realism."

The esthetic sense of the Martin sisters was furthermore influenced by moral and spiritual considerations. Céline always had a blind belief in the influence of prayer on talent, and failed to see they were in two different areas of reality. She recognized her lack of formal training before entering the convent, and she adopted the Blessed Virgin as her teacher of art and attributed all her progress to her influence. "Every time I took my pencils or brushes in hand, even when I had not used them for some time, I found that my facility had increased. Father Dubosq, who is rather reserved in his praise, encouraged me by saying that I drew perfectly. I thanked the Blessed Virgin for this, since I was well aware that I owe everything to her."

The nuns of Lisieux believed that any artistic work found its justification in the good accomplished for souls, regardless of its artistic deficiencies. This was the thinking of the time and environment in which they lived. They read only edifying books, and, for the most part, saw only portraits of the saints; thus, they somewhat resembled those primitive peoples who used paintings and drawings only for religious purposes. When they did a portrait of someone whom they considered a model of conduct and a vessel of grace, they relegated artistic authenticity to a secondary place and religious considerations predominated. A religious picture was evaluated by a special set of norms, and only when a picture contained no religious element was there consideration of ordinary esthetic values.

It was not until the end of the last century that art was able to gain complete autonomy. Rémy de Gourmont wrote in 1899: "Art has an individual and egoistic purpose. It will not deliberately serve any cause, whether it be religious or social or moral. It wants to be free, without performing any mission, and taking any direction it wants." By contrast, such a position clarifies the problem of St. Thérèse's portraits, and suggests that it is impossible to solve it by purely esthetic evaluation since we are in a situation which is beyond esthetics.

The unquestioned good which the portraits of Thérèse would accomplish relegated all questions of their artistic value or their psychological truth to a secondary place. Mother Marie of the Angels, prioress at the time, wrote to Msgr. de Teil in Feb. 1909, when the Process was being prepared: "Every day numerous letters assure us that these illustrations are a form of apostolate in accomplishing good for souls." And Thérèse's sister,

Marie, later confided to Léonie, with some bitterness: "If we had listened to our poor, late uncle, who disagreed with us, there would have been no portraits published in Thérèse's autobiography, and we now know that those portraits performed conversions and miracles."

Nevertheless, the Martin sisters did not identify the beautiful with the good. When Céline was relating the story of a servant of theirs who had been converted by her painting of Mary Magdalene, she added wryly: "That painting was just a lot of daubing, which proves that when God wants to touch a human heart he would rather use a work where love had directed the brush than a work of art. Which is precisely what happened with that canvas." Writing to Léonie in 1921 about a "Crucifixion" she had painted, she made this moving statement: "Pray God it will accomplish good. I have done it with such love, and I should so like Him to use it as a means to reach souls. Despite my efforts, there are undoubtedly mistakes in the anatomy, and experts will think I am unskillful, but I do not feel that is important and it will certainly be no impediment to God's grace." Provided good is accomplished, the rest matters little!

Today, we think more is necessary, because we are attempting to pursue good aims without abandoning artistic values.

Mme. Courtin-Duroux, a prominent French psychologist, who carefully compared twenty of the retouched photographs with the originals, arrived at this conclusion: "Céline, quite unconsciously, I am sure, has blurred the structural and psychological meaning of her sister's features by her retouching of the photographs."

The photographs in this album show a relaxed Thérèse, very much at ease, despite the tension caused by the long pose. She is concerned only with being, and she "is," in the fullest meaning of that word. Céline's retouching, on the contrary, places the emphasis on "appearing." Unwittingly, for there is no question of any malice on Céline's part, she has made Thérèse appear like the traditional picture of a saint. This can be seen in the contrast between the November 1896 photograph of Thérèse as sacristan and Céline's interpretation of it. In the original, she is sad; it was taken in November 1896, and she is aware that her death is imminent, and spiritual darkness haunts her. But, under Céline's pencil, she becomes a saint, the very image of perfection. The mouth, the entrance for earthly nourishment, is made smaller, the chin less prominent, while the eyes are much enlarged. She has become so celestial that it is difficult to realize she is still on earth.

When Thérèse played the role of St. Joan of Arc, her attitude was quite different, as she identified herself with the character to such an extent that her facial structure almost became like that of St. Joan. Céline's retouching lengthened Thérèse's face, thereby robbing it of its strength. She is made to appear like a child dressed up as Joan of Arc to take part in a parish play.

The impression of determination and strength emanating from Thérèse's photographs is, as a whole, destroyed by the retouching. Her strength of will, which is basically a control of all one's facilities, is converted into a superficial effort and straining. And the careful art work done on the photographs to idealize Thérèse only serves, by a curious revenge, to make her appear uneasy, rigid, and sometimes even tense. In the first pose of the retouched Gombault negative, her face is taut and all naturalness has disappeared, and the lily in her hands is made so stiff it resembles a rod. In all of the retouched pictures Thérèse appears less in command of herself, much more dependent on people around her, and quite susceptible to any suggestion. She seems only a little girl who wishes to be pleasant and nice to everybody.

The retouchings, by leaving her face devoid of any distinguishing characteristics, have also eliminated the mark of intelligence so evident in the original negatives. For example, the ninth photograph in this album, a group picture of the four Martin sisters and Mother Marie de Gonzague, shows Thérèse with an expression of extraordinary presence and composure, but the retouching makes her face a blank.

It takes courage to make these remarks. But they are less a criticism of Céline than a criticism of an age which sacrificed realism to idealism and thus involved itself in the artificial. Céline was not by temperament an idealist, and hence the art form she was compelled to practice only nullified her native talent. Had she received adequate training, her gift of observation and her sense of reality would have enabled her to leave us an artistic message of permanent validity.

VI.
Praise and Blame

Céline's paintings of Thérèse have been the object of both praise and criticism. For the past sixty years they have been a veritable sign of contradiction. There was even controversy about them among Thérèse's own contemporaries.

Of course, the Carmelite nuns who lived with St. Thérèse claimed they found a better resemblance of her in the paintings than in the original photographs. Sister Marie-Madeleine, a lay sister and a former novice of the Saint, actually shed tears when she first saw one of Céline's drawings in oval. "Oh, Sister Geneviève, how it resembles her this time," she said. "Don't do anything else to it. It's so realistic it seems as if I'm actually looking at her again." Mother Marie of the Angels, St. Thérèse's novice mistress, made the frequent statement: "The only painting I like is the one Céline did of our little Thérèse laid out after her death. It's the only one that really looks like Thérèse at the time of her burial."

Céline, whose artistic work had been praised in her own religious circle, was never able to understand how anyone could question the opinion of people who lived with Thérèse and said the paintings were fine representations of her. It was a kind of scandal to her, as she indicates in her private papers: "I cannot understand how people who have never even known St. Thérèse are able to doubt the good faith of her sisters. It's perfectly legitimate to question the talent of the painter, but not the judgment of her relatives about whether or not a painting resembled her." This argument was so forceful that it has been adopted by such distinguished authors as Petitot, Combes, and many others. In 1935, Jacques d'Arnoux wrote to Mother Agnes: "I find it strange and unconvincing that some people pretentiously claim they know more about the character, and even the physical traits, of St. Thérèse than the Carmel of Lisieux where God has preserved her own sisters for us."

However, even this argument is challenged by the extensive documentation I have had at my disposal. My research revealed that members of the Guérin family and other contemporaries of Thérèse objected to Céline's paintings, preferring instead the actual photographs. The Guérins were so hostile to the paintings that Mother Marie of the Angels, prioress of the Carmel, felt obliged to warn Msgr. de Teil about it before his visit to Lisieux. "You will receive hospitality at the home of M. Guérin, Sister Thérèse's uncle," she wrote. "But we all feel rather badly that, despite his great love for Thérèse, he has all sorts of prejudices against her autobiography, and he communicates these prejudices to his daughter and to his son-in-law, Doctor La Néele, who live with him. He is continually objecting to the illustrations in the book, and yet we published them only after we had asked advice from competent people."

Jeanne Guérin and Doctor La Néele liked the photographs of Abbé Gombault, and began to distribute them quietly. Of course, no one is a prophet nor an artist in his own family, and in addition, there existed a certain incompatibility of character between Céline Martin and her cousin, Jeanne Guérin. St. Thérèse alludes to this in her autobiography when she remarks wryly: "The two older girls, who never shared the same opinion about anything, argued all the way home." However, there is no reason to suspect the honesty of Doctor La Néele's opinion, and he expressed it with quite some vigor. "Francis came to the parlor on business the other day," Céline wrote to Léonie in 1913, "and he scolded all of us, especially me, claiming that none of my portraits resembled Thérèse. He also said he had Abbé Gombault's photograph enlarged, and it was the only one he cared to see circulated." M. Guérin also had enlarged and distributed the photograph of Thérèse in the convent courtyard. Céline discussed this subject again with Léonie in a letter of 1917 when she reported that her cousin Jeanne promised not to distribute these photographs any more but still refused to destroy them. "I know she allows these photographs we dislike so much to be reproduced by anyone who requests it," she wrote. But after Doctor La Néele's death Jeanne broke down in tears when she begged Céline's forgiveness for the pain her attitude and that of her husband had caused.

Another of Thérèse's contemporaries, Mother Saint-Léon from the Abbey in Lisieux, wrote about the Gombault photograph in a letter to Abbé

Robin, dated in 1933: "The picture of Thérèse as a novice with that nice smile looks just like her. I have it also on postcards—one retouched and the other unretouched, so they can be compared. This way you are sure of knowing the truth."

Are we, then, forced to make a decision about these contradictory opinions, or can we simply record them in the tradition of historians who quite frequently discover conflicting testimony about even the smallest matters? We can say, at least, that the conflict of opinion about this photograph was caused by two distinct visions of reality. The nuns of Carmel in their enclosed environment were subjected to the influence of a literature and an imagery in which, little by little, the ideal supplanted the real. They also fashioned among themselves a kind of common recollection of Thérèse in which they projected their own feelings and memories. On the other hand, Doctor La Néele, his wife, and Mother Saint-Léon were more inclined to a realism which was certainly more authentic, but at the same time somewhat limited—for, after all, the Gombault photograph, interesting as it might have been, was not a definitive picture of Thérèse since her face was still in the process of transition.

If Céline's portraits aroused controversy among the members of her family and among her own contemporaries, we should not be surprised that they have been hotly discussed throughout the world. They have certainly had an amazing distribution, a diffusion due, perhaps in God's special plan, to the fact that they conformed to the tastes of the times. As Abbé Robin notes, "A painted portrait was needed to popularize this young saint, one which was somewhat conventional and perhaps a little too pretty, but executed with great tenderness. It was necessary to depict those thornless roses and those artificial decorations which have so amused the sophisticated."

These pictures enjoyed an unparalleled success. "We were never able to catch up with all the requests we received from the faithful," Mother Agnes sighed at the Apostolic Process. Sister Marie of the Trinity, whose bright and cheerful face enlivens some of the group pictures of the community, had charge of the business arrangements with manufacturers of the pictures and medals, and she continually refused to allow agents to distribute the pictures because the distribution took care of itself. The Process records that 8,046,000 pictures were printed in France from 1898 to 1915. During the First World War a great number of soldiers, even those who were not particularly devout, carried a colored picture of this appealing saint. An aviator painted her picture on the wings of his plane, and a navigator placed it in his cabin.

Of course, the reports of visions always maintained that Thérèse was incomparably more beautiful than her picture. Roger Lefèvre, a wounded soldier who claimed he was assisted by St. Thérèse on the battlefield, replied to a question about whether Thérèse was beautiful: "Oh, yes! Much more beautiful than her pictures."

St. Thérèse, however, has utilized these pictures to introduce herself to people all over the world, spreading her influence to jungle huts and nomad tents and Eskimo igloos. For this reason, at least, Céline's portraits merit our respect. They will always remain part of a religious tradition, and they will continue to command the interest of future ages. It is quite true, as Claudel says, that God's plan for the salvation of souls includes "the enthusiasm and honest effort of an artist who, in whatever manner and doing his best with the means at his disposal, tries not to project himself but to *respond* to a word by a word, to a question by a deed, and to the Creator by a work of creativity."

Some years ago, Father Petitot, the theologian, wrote: "If this famous portrait of the Saint, which arouses so much interest and enthusiasm, has been able to stimulate the conversion of souls, it is because the picture is at once tranquil and profound."

Despite this general enthusiasm, however, the voices of critics and people of greater discernment were soon heard. The writer, Lucie Delarue Mardrus, thus describes Thérèse: "She had the forehead of a mystic, strong cheek bones, determined Norman chin and jaw, a sensitive artist's nose, and the mouth of a lively but disciplined person. And under her stubborn eyebrows, her eyes have an intense and reserved look which combines intelligence, strength, and self-mastery."

Photographs unauthorized by the Carmel were soon distributed in great numbers. These were negatives, it must be noted, which were dishonestly made from prints of the original pictures, then clumsily reproduced and issued for circulation. The third pose of the photographs taken on June 7, 1897, was the print from which many of these counterfeits were made. "This was the last good picture taken of Thérèse before her death," the Carmel explained later. "Soon after her death it was given to some of her relatives and friends. It was even used to illustrate the first edition of the *Autobiography,* but we were not satisfied with the result. The picture was then distributed without our permission. Rephotographed, enlarged, excessively retouched, this picture was the origin of innumerable unauthorized reproductions which were as untrue as they were varied."

Hence, the indignation of the Saint's sisters who failed to recognize Thérèse's features or her expression in these new photographs. They considered them completely inaccurate, and consequently came to believe that the photographs they themselves had retouched were faithful representations because they seemed to correspond with their own recollections of Thérèse. The nuns were convinced they were serving the cause of good, although they sometimes did so in a hostile way, especially Céline who had always lived up to her childhood nickname, "the fearless one." Ecclesiastical authorities tried to mollify the angered nuns, advising them to ignore the new photographs and practice holy indifference, but the advice was not always followed. In 1923, Canon Dubosq wrote to the Carmel: "Believe me, there would be no end of work and anxiety for you and me if we try to respond to all the objections which have been raised in this matter, and even at that it would be quite useless. You cannot stop people from chattering, finding fault, offering opinions, judging, pronouncing, suspecting, no more than you could stop a river from flowing down a mountain. For some time now the story has been circulated that the pretty photographs of Sister Thérèse with the large eyes and face formed in a perfect oval are nothing more than compositions which have been corrected, retouched, and idealized by the enthusiastic love of her artist sister. This has been said by relatives, by former acquaintances, by this one, and by that one, by someone from Lisieux, from Caen, from Alençon, etc., etc. This question is being widely discussed, and nothing we can do will stop it. Nor should we be surprised at it, because people who are interested in Sister Thérèse want to know about these things and find the answer. I shall continue to offer an explanation every time I get the opportunity; but as for preventing people from chattering about it . . . it's like trying to stop washerwomen from gossiping about their neighbor."

Canon Dubosq's attitude was a prudent one, although a bit on the defensive side, but it did not offer any real solution. And because the question remained largely unsolved, the discussion grew more bitter from commentator to commentator—Ghéon, for example, compared the retouchings to "sickening syrup"; and Etienne Robo provoked a furor in the English-speaking world by a book questioning the authenticity of the portraits in which certain gratuitous and biased statements were made.

It would be unfair to blame the Carmel for all the horrible manufactured products which have been modeled on Céline's paintings and which can still be found in the windows of stores selling "religious articles." We are not in the realm of art, but of commerce. A store counter full of these mass-produced objects gives a cheap illusion of art, and the people who manufacture them think they are justified since there is a ready market for them. Thus, Thérèse's image has become standardized in French churches and those of the entire world. The statue of Thérèse continually showering roses has taken its place beside St. Michael conquering the dragon, and St. Joan of Arc unfurling her banner, and the Curé of Ars smiling tirelessly. The poverty of the Thérèsian imagery is merely an illustration of the poverty of religious art at the beginning and the middle of this century. Manufacturers, both Christian and non-Christian, have not failed to take this opportunity of making further strides along the much-traveled road of ugliness and misrepresentation. In addition to the pious articles, they have used colored pictures of St. Thérèse with her roses on other manufactured objects for secular use: tablecloths, inkstands, cider jugs, flowerpots, thermometers, snuffboxes.

The wonder is that God should make use of these shoddy articles, these artistic sins, to accomplish His work of grace. Paul Claudel, writing about the statues in the shops of the Place Saint-Sulpice, expresses it magnificently: "This infantry of Saint-Sulpice, all these soldiers of Christ who were born of their mothers' flesh and blood, who were reanimated with the fire of grace, and who are now made out of butter by the manufacturers of the rue Bonaparte; all these cocoanut St. Josephs and those depressing St. Thérèses—how many fervent prayers have they heard, how much piety have they aroused, how much consolation have they given, how much repentance and sacrifice have they caused, how many prayers to God have they carried aloft, and of how many graces have they been the instrument?"

Some people take the rather peculiar position that these horrible works of religious art can show us, even in their ugliness, more of God's Beauty than real works of art which ignore God and concentrate on man. André Frossard, that lover of paradox, has recently written, "The ugliness of a pious object is an indirect witness to supernatural beauty which actually defies description. The honeyed statues of St. Thérèse which appear in our parish churches bring prayer to the lips immediately."

Indeed! But since we cannot arm ourselves with a whip of cords before entering the Temple, let us follow the sage advice of Canon Dubosq: "I have seen all kinds of unbelievable things—brochures, images, everything. What shall we do about it, then? Nothing! We must endure it. As the cult and admiration of our dear little Sister spreads, we shall see more and more merchandising of those horrible portraits which are only caricatures of Thérèse. We shall see pictures brightly painted in canary yellow and Prussian blue. Believe me, Sister Thérèse would laugh at them heartily. You can no more stop this business than you could stop birds from eating the cherries in a garden by putting a padlock on the gate."

I am sure that Thérèse, who was unconcerned about her habit being a bit askew and who sometimes spoke of her body as an unimportant covering and who was indifferent to her own prettiness, must laugh when she sees how she has been depicted. Perhaps this disguise of her true personality was permitted so that she might hide herself even more completely, as she expressed it on the eve of her profession when she reflected on the Holy Face: "I shall be the spouse of Him whose face was hidden and unrecognized." Yet, by means of these various representations, she was able to "do good upon the earth." This, above all else, is what she wanted.

VII.
Official Statements about the Photographs

THIS STUDY would be incomplete if it failed to discuss the official statements about the photographs which have been prompted by the Carmel.

As we mentioned above, the eighth edition of *The Story of a Soul* in 1907 contained a note about the physical appearance of St. Thérèse, although the text seemed to be borrowed from Ribera, the biographer of St. Teresa of Avila.

The 1924 edition presents for the first time a statement by Bishop Lemonnier of Lisieux about the portraits of Sister Thérèse of the Infant Jesus. It accompanies another statement by the Bishop concerning the authenticity of the texts published in *The Story of a Soul,* and the somewhat uncomfortable admission is made that editorial work was done on the original manuscripts.

Bishop Lemonnier's remarks are based on an inquiry he conducted at the Carmel where he examined twelve to fifteen photographs, mainly group pictures of the nuns taken from 1895 to 1897. His examination of the photographs brought him to the conclusion that the Saint lost her natural composure when she had to pose. He then advised the continued use of the oval half-length drawing of Thérèse, seeing in it "a very conscientious and careful synthesis of the most expressive aspects of the aforementioned photographs." "This is why," he adds, "we have not the least bit of hesitancy in calling this a *true and authentic portrait* of the Servant of God at about the age of twenty-three."

This same thesis was stated in 1926 in a booklet entitled *A propos des Portraits de Sainte Thérèse de l'Enfant-Jésus,* a publication of the Office Central in Lisieux. This booklet is only twenty pages in length, and it contains seven pages of photographs plus a brief commentary. There is a three-page preface by Canon Dubosq, Vicar General and superior of the Major Seminary of Bayeux, in which he recalls and summarizes the statement of Bishop Lemonnier mentioned above. The preface claims that Céline's compositions and retouched photographs "were not done to present an imaginary idealization, but rather to offer a conscientious and careful synthesis of the many untouched photographs in the Carmel's possession." Canon Dubosq notes that criticism continued, despite the Bishop's statement, and it disquieted the followers of St. Thérèse. The booklet prints some of the photographs which had been called into question, and Canon Dubosq comments: "Absolutely no retouching was done on the faces; the only things corrected were the arrangement of the hair or some details about the clothing."

A new booklet was published by the Office Central in 1949, *Sur l'authenticité des Portraits de Sainte Thérèse de l'Enfant-Jésus,* based on Abbé Combes' study of the photographs in his *Saint Thérèse and Suffering.* It states: "This remarkable study of the photographs of St. Thérèse should remove all doubts about the photographs corrected by the Carmel, and it offers evidence to show they should be considered completely authentic."

The booklet contains information on the three poses of June 7 and compares the shape of the face in the third pose of that date with the oval portrait used as a frontispiece in the autobiography and which was declared authentic by the Diocesan Tribunal at the Process of Canonization.

When Canon Dubosq entered the discussion of the photographs, therefore, he based his argument on the authority of Bishop Lemonnier. But since the Bishop's statement was offered without any textual proof, the 1926 booklet sought to prove its point by comparing the more important photographs of Thérèse, principally the poses of June 7, with the official portraits issued by the Carmel and also, by way of contrast, with the highly imaginative pictures which were circulated unofficially. The 1949 booklet follows the same line of argument. The thesis never changes: a defense of Céline's oval portrait, and the argument that it is authentic. It is described as a "synthetic portrait," made after a study of the best elements of the subject's natural and habitual expression.

The term "synthetic portrait" which is used so frequently in the discussion of Céline's compositions has raised strong protests in literary and artistic circles. However, the concept of a portrait-synthesis is not quite so foolish as it sounds, because even before the advent of photography painters tried to produce a combination of fleeting, and sometimes differing, expressions of the same face. La Tour, for example, attempted to select the most indicative expressions from "the two hundred faces" of the man he was studying, and he admitted that the choice demanded a terrible labor of synthesis on his part.

Had Céline possessed La Tour's talent, her long association with Thérèse would have enabled her to produce a work which would have compelled our respect, and her synthesis would have been universally accepted. We owe her a debt of gratitude, at any rate, for taking the numerous photographs of Thérèse—which she could not greatly have disliked since she always carried with her a little proof of the second pose of the photograph of June 7, 1897. Moreover, it was she who chose the 1896 photograph of Thérèse with the lilies as frontispiece for the unedited *Autobiography*. We must beg her pardon for the paradoxical situation in which she involves us, because it is only by studying her photographs that we can criticize her paintings.

VIII.
The Present Edition

THE PHYSICAL COMPOSITION of this volume would have required no decisions at all if it had been published fifty years ago. Even the most honest publishing venture would have retained only the "suitable" photographs, and they would have been retouched and cropped into the same familiar and monotonous pattern. Today, however, we strive to achieve two apparently contradictory goals: an absolutely authentic presentation of the documents, and an arrangement which is as artistic as possible. The decisions we have made in publishing this volume attempt to serve this twofold ideal.

Since this album had to be, first of all, authentic, we had to present the forty-seven photographs exactly as they are, without any kind of retouching or even repairing, and we had to retain all the faulty negatives, which do, nevertheless, have historical value. The negatives are all authentic, although they are of different kinds: original plates, secondary plates obtained by contact with the original, citrate proofs made by the contact process, and some plates which had been retouched but were chemically cleaned of the retouchings (this occurred in only four instances). The pictures are presented in their original size, or, in some cases, what we presume to be the original size; for example, enlargements from which the retouching was removed are reduced to a $9/12$ or $13/18$ size, which was the usual size at the time those photographs were taken.

We have attempted to present the photographs in their chronological order. Some of the plates have a date annotated on them, while the dates of others can be ascertained by a reference in some other document or by the very scenes depicted: a profession, a community feast, etc. Sometimes the costume worn in the picture helps the historian to discover the date: a postulant, for example, is dressed differently from a novice or a professed nun. Céline's white veil in photographs 18 to 25 proves they were taken before her profession, at which time she received the black veil. The state of the trees and bushes in the chestnut walk inside the Carmel can also supply information. Other points of reference were the folds of the cloaks, and the arrangement of the veils or of the toque (the white linen headband). A Carmelite has many different ways of putting in the pins to make the folds of the toque and Thérèse pinned hers in various ways at different times.

Pictures are dated as alternate poses of the same subject when there is a serious presumption that they were taken at the same time. Multiple posing on the same occasion was done in the Carmel so as not to waste time and to utilize the free time on a particular feast day to the best advantage. Céline tried to practice economy in developing the pictures, and the carriage of her camera contained two plates which were ordinarily developed simultaneously.

Applying these principles, we have displayed the photographs in what we feel is a competent chronological order in successive pages throughout the album. This satisfies the historical demands in the album.

The enlargements that accompany each original are included in order to give a better idea of the original photograph. In the French edition, the Paris technicians, at our request, repaired some tears and scratches on the negatives after they had reproduced these negatives in their actual condition. For the English language edition, however, these imperfections have been retained in order to preserve authenticity rather than satisfy esthetic demand.

The pages that follow, therefore, form a kind of photographic commentary on the photographs in their original state and size. Our civilization is a pictorial one where the illustration is more and more supplanting the written word, where television, picture magazines, and illustrations are gaining greater importance. We should, therefore, utilize the modern artistic procedures to allow the reader an intuitive and immediate contact with Thérèse of Lisieux—enlargements of her face, detail sections of the various photographs, views of her hands, all arranged in a free and natural pattern. These pages permit one to study the photographs more easily, and perhaps to be more forcefully struck by a particular attitude of the body or a feature of the face. And does not the human face, more than anything else, tell us the most about a person? Even those who might at first be surprised and disturbed by the enlargements must admit that they give immediacy and direct contact. Furthermore, the enlargement and cutting of the photographs were not done arbitrarily: the technical quality of the photograph was taken into account as much as the subject itself or its dramatic value.

Sometimes Thérèse's veil is used as a background framing her face. Other times only her face is shown, while the veil and everything else is cut away. In this way, Thérèse's face escapes from its milieu and historical setting and becomes timeless. We have enlarged some pictures excessively so that we can study the material and structure of the face at closer range; in some of these enlargements we were also able to present, one by one, enlarged pictures of Thérèse's sisters.

We witnessed the most moving reaction to the photographs at the Carmel itself. We wondered how the nuns, who had for years grown accustomed to a particular image of Thérèse, would react to such a revolutionary undertaking. Their instant and unanimous approval was proof to us that we had actually unearthed the essential and that truth had emerged with compelling force.

ARE THE DOCUMENTS assembled in this album of historical importance?

Admittedly, we have very little exact knowledge of the earthly faces of the saints of the past. Certainly, Byzantine mosaics and medieval frescoes do not tell us much about their individual characteristics. Nor is the art of portraiture which appeared around the Renaissance era always reliable. A real game of hide-and-seek seems to have been played out between great artists and the great personages they have portrayed, especially when these personages were saints.

For one portrait of Thomas More or of John Fisher by Hans Holbein, there are many mediocre works executed by painters of scant talent and retouched afterward in a shocking manner. True, it was often necessary to wait until a saint died, and sometimes even until his body was exhumed, to depict his likeness; it is hard for us to consider these interpretations as always trustworthy. And rarely does the copy of a portrait or a document, even when declared authentic, receive the full approval of contemporaries.

On the whole more disappointment and fault-finding than approval are recorded in history. When he looked at a portrait of Teresa of Avila by Juan de la Miseria, Father Gracián exclaimed: "That is the picture we have of our Mother! We wish it were more in keeping with reality, for she had a charming face and one that inspired piety in the beholder." The Jesuits, on seeing a portrait of Ignatius of Loyola made several hours after his death, declared: "No, that is not our Father!"

Even death masks, so greatly prized for their apparent exactness before the invention of photography, are very deceiving. Strictly speaking, they do not give us the likeness of the living person, but a face in process of transition.

Must we resign ourselves to the lack of authenticity in such portraits and even rejoice to see the veracity of documents once more placed in question? The earthly face is, after all, but a covering, a mask of little importance in comparison with the soul.

But then why do the features of the face reflect the soul? Thérèse of

Lisieux herself was convinced of this, for she said: "The face is the reflection of the soul . . . you are constantly in the sight of God and of the angels." And La Tour wrote of his models: "They believe I copy only the lines of their faces but, although they are unaware of it, I reach down to the very depth of their being and I show them as a whole." And is there not some reason behind the surprising conclusions of present-day psychologists?

If there is an atom of truth in physical matter we should take it into account, for too often half-truths have canceled it out. It is not only the saints' earthly faces that are little known to us, but also their lives. The edifying biographies of the past, fearing to belittle even slightly the admirable beings held up for the imitation of the faithful unfortunately have been sources of falsities and have also contained serious omissions. To hide the truth even in part is often to propagate falsehood. And if the model which is held up is false, how much more false are the imitations of that model? Many souls have been set on wrong paths in their search for the Kingdom of God by having tried to copy to the letter an example placed before them which never existed. The imitation of saints stripped of the adornments and the infirmities of their human nature often leads to hypocritical formalism or discouragement.

Does a remedy exist for what has happened in the past? In certain cases the discovery of documents and the progress of psychological science enable us to rectify our opinions.

In the preparation of this album, absolute honesty has been our criterion. Because of the unusual number of photographs in existence we feel we have been able to make a saint come alive again in her actual milieu.

Fr. François de Saint-Marie, O.C.D.

THE PORTRAITS

Cᴇʀᴛᴀɪɴ of the authentic photographs in this album have been previously published. However, even when not retouched, they may be found to vary in clearness or in expressions from the photos shown here due to the differing methods of reproduction.

Although Céline arranged the groups for the photographs and focused the camera, it was usually some other nun who snapped the actual picture. Sister St. John of the Cross frequently served as the operator (see, for example, photo 18).

When there are fewer than five figures in the groups, the names of the nuns are given in the text of the commentary. Otherwise, their identity is indicated by diagrams carrying numbers which refer to the list of nuns given at the end of the album (p. 222). A list of locations where the pictures were taken is also given (p. 224), and is followed by a plan of the convent and grounds of the Carmel of Lisieux.

In each case the original photograph is the first to appear under each number.

CHRONOLOGICAL ORDER OF THE PORTRAITS

The numbers in this list correspond to those of the photographs reproduced in their original size.

1

1. THÉRÈSE AT THREE AND A HALF

This picture was taken in the middle of July, 1876, by a professional photographer in Alençon. The negative is not a glass one, but a very small citrate proof, 2 x 7/4 cm., obtained by contact process with a negative. We have presented it here in a size which is certainly close to the size of the original negative.

A letter from Mme. Martin to her daughter Pauline dated July 16, 1876, informs us that three successive poses had to be taken on that occasion be-cause Thérèse moved quite a bit during the taking of the picture. "Although she ordinarily had a happy expression on her face, she was pouting then because she was close to tears, and we had to keep encouraging her."

Thérèse was three and a half at the time of this picture. The Martin family was still living in Alençon, and Thérèse was enjoying the happy and untrammeled years of this first period of her life.

1A

1B

2

2. THÉRÈSE AT EIGHT WITH HER SISTER CÉLINE

Taken in 1881 by Besnier, a professional photographer in Lisieux. The size of the negative is 9 x 12 cm. In the retouched versions issued by the Carmel, Pauline had the bows on the dresses rearranged.

M. Martin never cared for this photograph. He felt that the photographer failed to show the foreheads clearly and there was too much shadow on top of the heads.

Thérèse, shown here with a jumping rope in her hand, was eight, while Céline was twelve. Thérèse's mother had died four years previously, and the Martin family moved to Lisieux shortly afterward. Her mother's death had been a profound blow for the young girl, and she was now enduring what she called her "winter of trial," a period of extreme sensitivity and unhappiness. This same year she entered the Benedictine Abbey school at Lisieux.

2A

2B

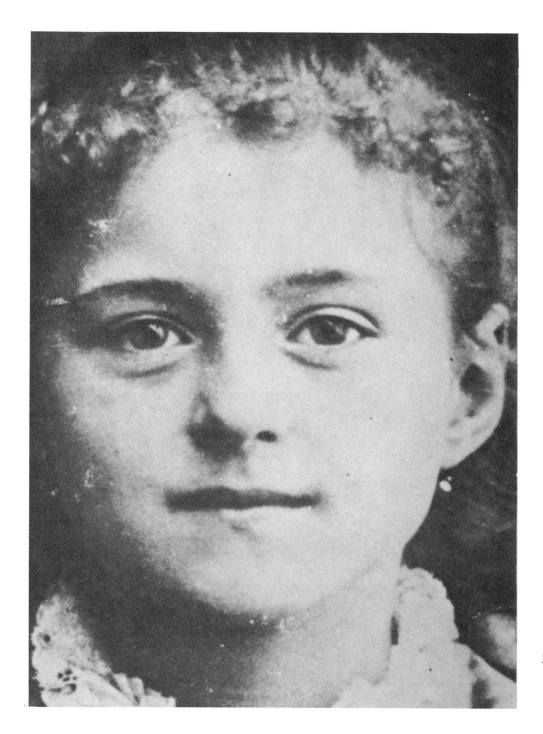

2C

2D

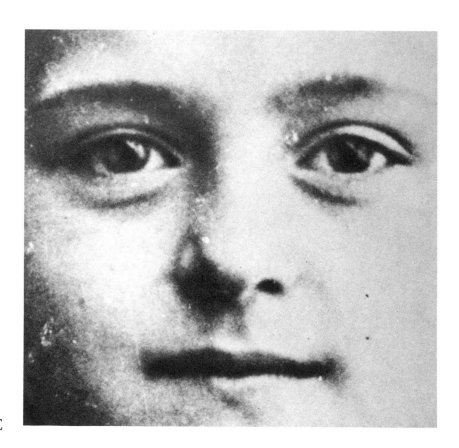

2E

3

3. THÉRÈSE AT THIRTEEN

The original negative of this February, 1886, photograph has been lost. The picture was discovered in a folder at the Carmel titled *Famille Martin: Sainte Thérèse et ses Sœurs,* a collection of photographs of members of the Martin family. The folder was given to the Carmel in 1917 by the family of the photographer, M. Pouet. The pictures were probably not reproduced from original plates, but from citrate proofs, and there are signs of faulty developing.

The original was probably a size 9 x 12 cm., but the photograph shown here is from a 28 x 7/35 x 2 enlargement which had been retouched by Céline in crayon and water colors. We restored this enlargement to its original condition through chemical processes.

Thérèse is thirteen years old in this picture. She has already been cured of the strange and crippling illness which struck her in 1883, and at the end of this year she was to experience her "Christmas conversion," that instant maturity which marked the end of her childhood sensitivity.

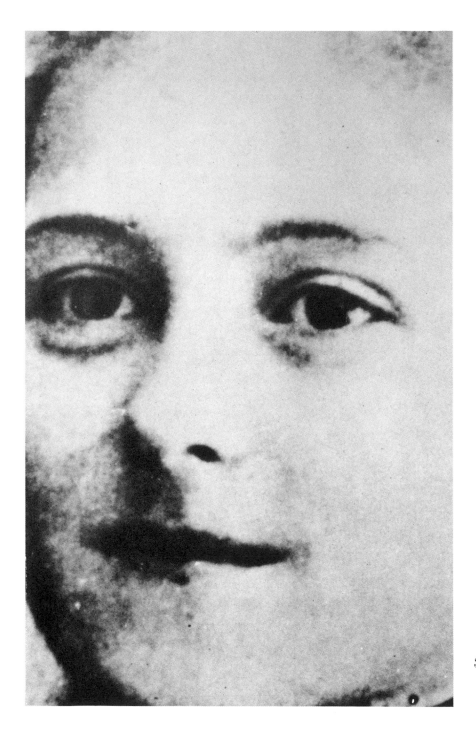

3B

4

4. THÉRÈSE AT FIFTEEN

Taken by Mme. Besnier, a professional photographer at Lisieux. The glass negative, size 9 x 12 cm., has a smear of paint running along Thérèse's shoulder. This blemish was removed in the many copies distributed by the Carmel since 1926.

She is photographed with her hair knotted on top of her head, the coiffure she adopted for the first time to make herself appear older when she visited Bishop Hugonin on October 31, 1887. Although it might appear that the picture was taken at that time, Céline's notes inform us it was taken in April, 1888, a few days before Thérèse's entrance into Carmel.

There had been some reluctance on the part of the ecclesiastical authorities to accepting so young a girl into the Carmel—hence, Thérèse's decision to abandon her usual long curls for her visit to the Bishop. While waiting for the Bishop's response, she went on a pilgrimage to Rome with her father during November and the early part of December. She entered Carmel on April 9, 1888, at the age of fifteen.

81

4A

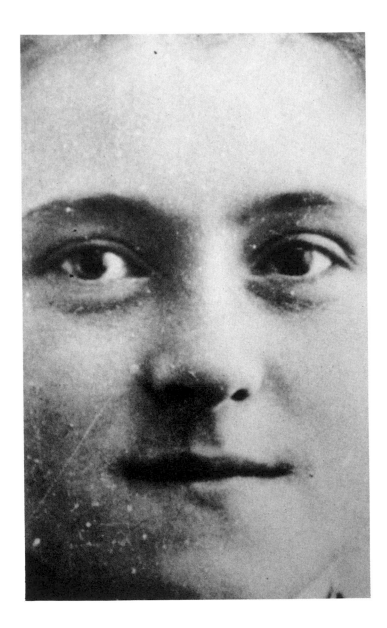

4B

CRUX,
AVE,
CARMELI.

5. THÉRÈSE AS A NOVICE IN WHITE MANTLE

Taken in January of 1889, some days after Thérèse's clothing with the religious habit, which occurred on January 10th of that year. The photographer was Abbé Gombault, bursar of the Minor Seminary, who had received permission to enter the Carmel to offer advice about the installation of gas light. The negative is glass, 13 x 18 cm., and several repatched needle holes can be found near the left cheek. The back of the negative has been painted red in order to emphasize the sky.

A January 1889 letter from Pauline to Céline and Léonie discusses this photograph: "... and above all, tell our dear father not to show the photographs to anybody except my uncle, and don't tell anyone that Abbé Gombault photographed the angel. People would think he entered the cloister just for that, which is not so, because the Bishop gave him permission to come with the contractor to visit the old house. (This secrecy is very *important*.)"

At the time of this picture, Thérèse had been in the convent for nine months, and was then sixteen years old.

5A

5B

6. THÉRÈSE AS A NOVICE WITHOUT MANTLE

Taken on the same occasion and by the same photographer as the preceding photo. Thérèse had just removed her white mantle, which can be seen folded on the porch railing behind the cross. The glass negative, 13 x 18 cm., is slightly scratched and repaired. A corner of the negative has been broken off, and then glued on again.

Abbé Gombault sent this photograph, as well as the preceding one, to the nuns for their own use. Only the first pose was used, since the second displeased the community, especially Marie who objected to it strenuously, claiming that the harsh light deformed Thérèse's features.

The negative of this second pose was returned to Abbé Gombault, but when consideration was being given to Thérèse's canonization, the Abbé began to receive many requests for the picture. The Carmel felt it was a poor picture of Thérèse, and asked the Bishop to recover the negative. Abbé Gombault, displeased by the request, had a second negative made from the original and sent this to the Carmel. He retained the original until his death, at which time it was returned to the Carmel.

A retouched version of the first pose (picture 5) was used in editions of *The Story of a Soul* after 1899, and a retouched version of the second (picture 6) was used in the 1922 *Vie en Images de Sainte Thérèse de l'Enfant-Jésus.*

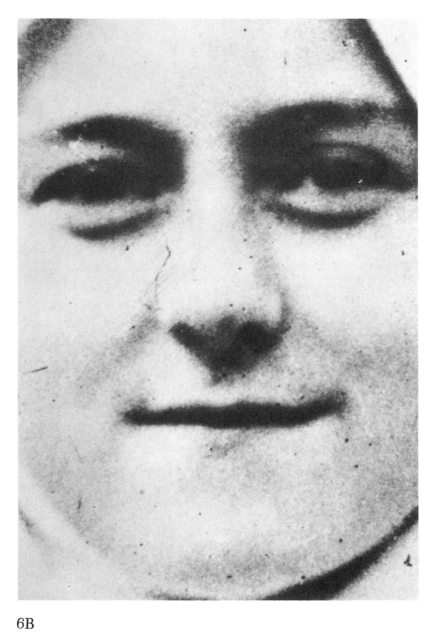

6B

6A

7. THÉRÈSE AND HER SISTERS WITH MOTHER MARIE DE GONZAGUE ON THE INFIRMARY PORCH

Taken in 1894, sometime after September 14, which was the date of Céline's entrance into the Carmel. This is probably the first picture taken with the camera Céline brought to the convent. The negative is glass, 13 x 18 cm. An inadequate washing of the negative has caused the loss of some gelatine and large acid marks. Sister St. Vincent de Paul, the white-veiled nun at the left, has scratch marks across her face.

The nuns in the photograph are, from left to right: Sister St. Vincent de Paul; Marie (Sister Marie of the Sacred Heart), Thérèse's eldest sister; Thérèse, leaning against a pillar of the infirmary porch; Mother Marie de Gonzague, the former prioress; and Pauline (Mother Agnes of Jesus), Thérèse's second eldest sister, who had become prioress of the Carmel in the preceding year.

Thérèse is twenty-one years old in this picture. Four years earlier she made her profession of vows, and at this time she was serving as mistress of novices.

7A

8. SISTER GENEVIÈVE NEAR THE INFIRMARY PORCH

This glass negative, 13 x 18 cm., was taken on the same day as the preceding photograph. The nuns who appeared in the preceding photograph have departed, and Céline, who was then a postulant, is standing alone near the stairs of the infirmary porch. Thérèse can be just seen from the back as she passes through the doorway. This photograph is used here merely as serving to indicate some of the sites in the Carmel. The ground floor windows on the right are those of the infirmary where Thérèse spent the last months of her life.

9

9. THÉRÈSE, HER SISTERS, AND MOTHER MARIE DE GONZAGUE IN THE COURTYARD OF THE LOURDES GROTTO—1st POSE

Taken in late 1894 or early 1895. One might object to this date on the grounds that Céline was wearing a novice's habit, which she actually received on February 5, 1895. However, her notes inform us that she had put on the novice's habit for this pose, perhaps to try it for size. At any rate, the photograph was taken between September 14, 1894, and February 5, 1895.

The negative is glass, 13 x 18 cm. The gelatine was cracked during a recent washing, and thus the negative is veined like marble. Fortunately Thérèse's face was little damaged.

The nuns are seated in the Lourdes grotto. The grotto no longer exists in the Carmel today, but it was near the site of the present chapel where Thérèse's body is now kept. The nuns in the photograph seem weary and strained. Thérèse appears somewhat distant and a little sad. She faces Mother Marie de Gonzague, and the comparison of the two physiognomies is quite interesting.

After Thérèse's death, Sister Marie of the Incarnation, a lay sister, conceived the idea of cutting the picture of Thérèse seated on the bench from this photograph and pasting it on a photograph of the convent cemetery. This is the origin of the picture "Thérèse in meditation in the monastery garden" which can be found in different editions of *The Story of a Soul* from 1902.

This picture also served as the inspiration for Céline's oval portrait of Thérèse. The oval portrait was then superimposed on the body of Thérèse sitting in the garden, which, in addition to other retouching, explains the number of variations of this picture.

The nuns in the photograph are: Céline and Pauline (standing); Mother Gonzague, Marie, and Thérèse (seated).

9A

9B

100

9C

9D

10

10. THÉRÈSE, HER SISTERS, AND MOTHER MARIE DE GONZAGUE IN THE COURTYARD OF THE LOURDES GROTTO—2ND POSE

Taken on the same day and in the same place as the preceding photograph. The Carmel felt the picture was unsuccessful, and about a quarter of the original negative was cut away. Then Mother Marie de Gonzague's picture was eradicated from the group. Finally the whole negative was destroyed.

The photograph presented here comes from a citrate proof of the original negative. Retouching had been done on this proof in water colors: Mother Gonzague's picture was eliminated, the toques and veils were rearranged, the prioress' key carried by Pauline was made less obvious. The retouchings have been chemically removed by experts, and the picture restored to its authentic condition.

Mother Gonzague is standing behind the group. The four Martin sisters in the picture are, from left to right: Marie, Céline, Thérèse, and Pauline.

11. THÉRÈSE IN THE ROLE OF JOAN OF ARC—1st POSE

Taken between January 21, 1895, and the spring of that same year. The negative is glass, 13 x 18 cm., and it bears scratches over Thérèse's left eye. The plate was mistakenly inverted when it was placed in the camera, thus the picture was reversed. We reversed it again in the printing process, and it is presented here in its proper position.

The photograph was taken outdoors in the sacristy courtyard, next to an old painted wooden statue of Our Lady of Providence which was said to have been a miraculous statue.

Thérèse wrote a play about St. Joan of Arc for Pauline's feast day, January 21, and then acted the second part of it with the novices before the entire community. The presentation was enthusiastically received by the nuns. The photographs of the dramatization could have been taken some weeks after the actual event. The nuns wore wigs over their toques and decorated their religious robes with costuming made of paper or cardboard by the novices. The Carmel distributed this picture to some of its friends.

Thérèse was twenty-two years old at the time of these pictures, and she had just started to write the first section of her autobiography.

The detail enlargement (11 B) was made before the accidental scratching of the negative.

11B

12A

12. THÉRÈSE IN THE ROLE OF JOAN OF ARC—2ND POSE

Taken under the same circumstances as the preceding picture. The glass negative is 13 x 18 cm.

The statue of the Blessed Virgin is clearer in this picture, but Thérèse's face is slightly blurred. Thérèse has turned toward the statue.

13

13. THÉRÈSE AS JOAN OF ARC IN PRISON

A 13 x 18 cm. glass negative taken at
the same time. Note the helmet placed
on the pile of bricks.

13A

13B

14A

14. THÉRÈSE AS JOAN OF ARC DURING HER VISION OF ST. MARGARET

Another 13 x 18 cm. picture in the same series. Céline, who played the role of St. Margaret, was then twenty-five years old. The picture appears to have been taken from a slightly lower angle.

15

15. THÉRÈSE AS JOAN OF ARC CROWNED IN HEAVEN

The negative of this picture has been lost. The only remnant extant is this one proof, a narrow citrate strip which shows Thérèse by herself. The picture was not focused properly, and the fragment is rather blurred. It was probably taken on the same date as the preceding pictures. The photograph must have been taken indoors, if we can judge from the background and the rug at Thérèse's feet.

15A

16

16. THE COMMUNITY AT RECREATION IN THE CHESTNUT WALK— 1st POSE

Taken sometime after February 5, 1895, since Céline received the habit on that date and the picture shows her dressed as a novice. It was probably taken near the end of March or the beginning of April, because examination under a magnifying glass reveals some leaves on the fourth chestnut tree from the left. The negative is glass, 13 x 18 cm., and the section around Thérèse has been damaged by the numerous prints made from it.

The community is gathered in the walk of the chestnut trees, which have been recently pruned. The majority of these trees are still standing, including the third tree from the right on which the word MOTHER can be seen. The hermitage of the Holy Face is behind the trees on the left, and the original cemetery of the convent is in the middle rear of the picture.

Pauline, who was then prioress, is seated at a table in the center of the group painting a picture. Mother Gonzague is seated on her right. Céline, on the other side, is working at an easel painting a picture of the Blessed Virgin. At the left of the picture, Sister St. Stanislas, assisted by the novice Sister Marie of the Trinity, is unfastening the stars from the costume of St. Margaret worn by Céline in the preceding photographs.

Thérèse, on the left side of the group, is repairing the Infant Jesus statue which was her charge in the convent. Her sister Marie stands beside her.

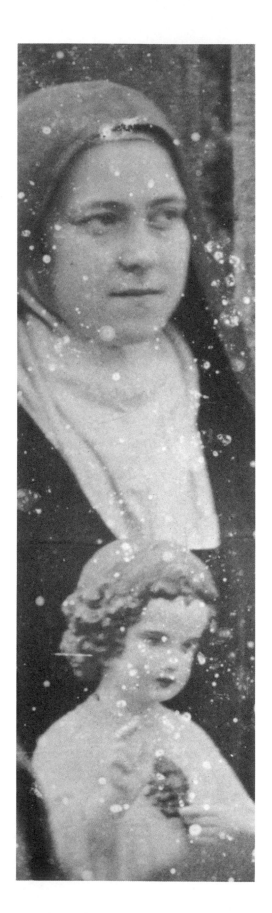

16A

16B

17

17. THE COMMUNITY AT RECREATION IN THE CHESTNUT WALK— 2ND POSE

Taken on the same occasion as the preceding photograph. This 13 x 18 cm. glass negative has defects similar to the other negative, but there are also many cracks in the gelatine.

Several of the nuns have changed places. Pauline is showing her finished painting to Mother Gonzague. The stars have already been removed from the costume of St. Margaret. The nun who is cutting bread on the right-hand side of the picture now holds a smaller piece in her hand.

Thérèse appears a little more stout in this photograph, which perhaps can be explained by the angle at which the picture was taken. However, Céline was very satisfied with this picture. "You see her as she was," she said.

This photograph was used in the 1953 edition of *The Story of a Soul*, and it was repaired when the cut was being prepared. In 1959, another more careful restoration of the picture was made on an enlargement, and widely distributed.

124

17A

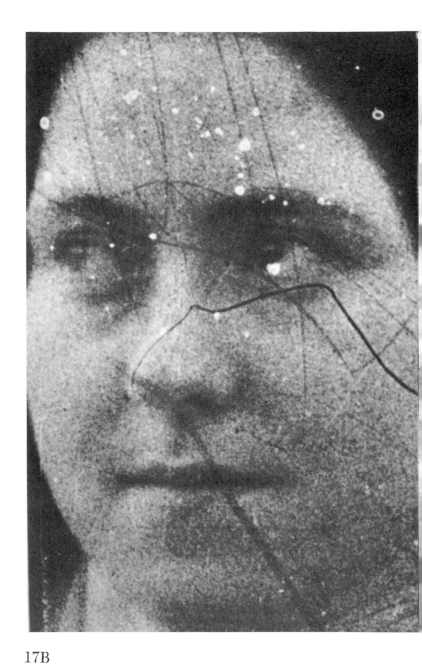

17B

18

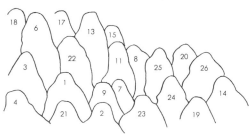

18. THE COMMUNITY ON THE CLOISTER PORCH

This photograph and the one following cannot be dated with any precision. They were both probably taken on the same day, sometime between Céline's investiture with the habit on February 5, 1895, and the end of July in the same year. In fact, Sister Anne of the Sacred Heart appears in both these pictures, and she departed for the Carmel of Saigon on July 29. The negative is glass, 13 x 18 cm.

The picture was taken in the interior courtyard of the convent. The cloister walk outside the refectory is at the left, and the cloister walk outside the choir is in the rear.

Several of the faces are blurred. The picture was taken from a slightly elevated angle, thus accentuating the width of Thérèse's chin.

On June 14th of this year Thérèse experienced her mystical wounding while making the Stations of the Cross.

18A

18B

19

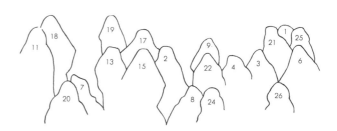

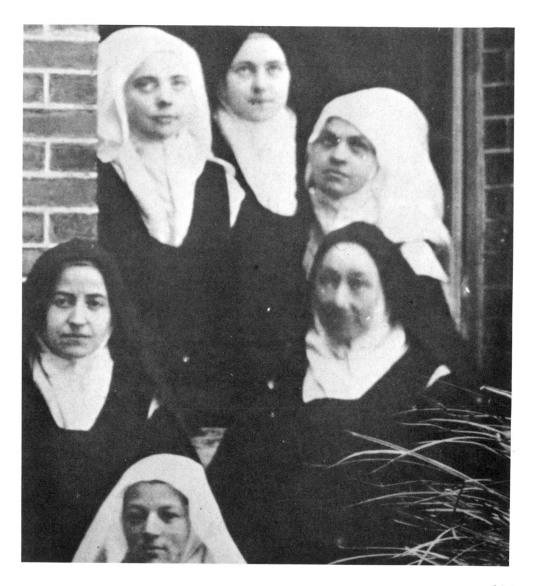

19A

19. THE COMMUNITY IN THE COURTYARD OF THE LOURDES GROTTO

This glass negative, 13 x 18 cm., was probably taken on the same day as the preceding one. A careful examination of the arrangement of the nuns' veils would seem to support this. Céline snapped and developed several nega-tives on a single occasion in order to save time and developing equipment, and each of her photographic carriers contained two plates. Several nuns moved during the pose and their faces are blurred.

20. THÉRÈSE WITH HER NOVICES AND MOTHER MARIE DE GONZAGUE AND MOTHER AGNES

This picture, which the Carmel has titled "Thérèse With Her Hourglass," was probably taken the same day as the two preceding ones. The negative is glass, 13 x 18 cm.

Mother Gonzague and Pauline are standing in the window. The novice on Thérèse's right is Sister Marie of the Trinity, and on her left, Sister Marthe and Céline. Sister Mary Magdalene is kneeling in front of the group. Thérèse has not pinned back her veil which makes it look different from the others, and also unbalances her face slightly.

This photograph was heavily retouched in publications released after the Second World War. A picture of Sister Marie of the Eucharist, Thérèse's cousin Marie Guérin, at that time a postulant, was inserted over the figure of Mother Gonzague; and a curtain was added to the window.

20A

20C

20B

21

21A

21. THE COMMUNITY GATHERED FOR THE FEAST OF THE GOOD SHEPHERD—1st POSE

Taken in 1895. We can date this picture precisely on either April 27th or 28th —the Saturday or Sunday of the Good Shepherd. A corner of this glass 13 x 18 cm. negative has been broken off at the bottom right. Some lines on the negative indicate that a shield was used to focus the picture directly on the group.

The community is grouped around Mother Agnes in the cloister garden. She holds in her hand a shepherd's staff decorated by the novices for this feast in honor of the superior. Thérèse is gazing at Céline. April 28th was Céline's birthday, and Thérèse had composed the "Song of Céline" for her first birthday in the convent.

22. THE COMMUNITY GATHERED FOR THE FEAST OF THE GOOD SHEPHERD—2ND POSE

Same date and occasion as the preceding picture. Glass negative, 13 x 18 cm.

Several of the nuns moved during the pose, and Thérèse's face is completely blurred.

23. THÉRÈSE WITH THE NOVICES AND THEIR SUPERIORS ON THE FEAST OF THE GOOD SHEPHERD

Taken on the same date as the two preceding photographs. The 13 x 18 cm. glass negative is cracked at the top.

The novitiate group is gathered around Mother Agnes who is still holding the shepherd's staff. The negative is scratched where Mother Agnes deliberately tried to eradicate her own picture, perhaps because she felt she appeared somewhat arrogant beside the dejected figure of Mother Gonzague.

Thérèse's face is heavily streaked.

23A

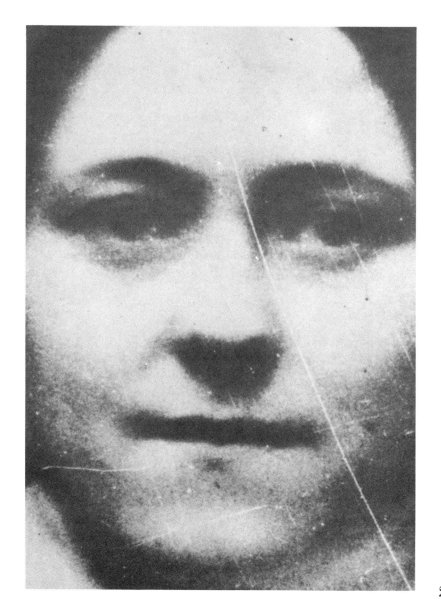

23B

24

24A

24. THE COMMUNITY AT THE LAUNDRY—1ST POSE

Taken sometime before the end of July, 1895. The negative is glass, 13 x 18 cm.

All of the nuns, with the exception of Sister Marie Emmanuel, who is standing at the extreme left, have removed the extra veil worn over their heads in the preceding photographs. They are wearing aprons, and they have rolled up their three sets of sleeves. During the actual washing at the convent, the nuns worked in relays, some doing the wash here in the laundry, while others took the clothes outside to thrash them with paddles like the one Thérèse holds in her hand. However, for this photograph they have all assembled in the laundry at the same time, which explains why they seem so crowded.

Thérèse's picture was taken from a higher angle, and thus the size of her forehead seems reduced and her face appears more oval.

24B

24C

25

25. THE COMMUNITY AT THE LAUNDRY—2ND POSE

This glass negative, 13 x 18 cm., was taken on the same day as the preceding picture.

The nuns have changed places for this second pose. Thérèse's face is completely blurred. We again see Sister Anne of the Sacred Heart (second kneeling figure from the left) who was scheduled to leave Lisieux at the end of July, 1895.

26

26. THÉRÈSE AND CÉLINE BENEATH THE CROSS IN THE CLOISTER COURTYARD

Taken March 17, 1896, the day on which Céline received the black veil. In previous releases of this picture, the Carmel attempted to simplify matters by giving the date of February 24, the day of Céline's profession. Céline's own face was heavily retouched in these earlier releases.

The original photograph has been lost, and the present picture is taken from a 49 x 59 cm. enlargement, heavily retouched in crayon and water colors by Céline. The picture has been chem- ically restored to its original condition. The handwritten title at the bottom of the picture reads: "Blessed Thérèse of the Infant Jesus kneeling beside her sister Céline, Sister Geneviève of the Holy Face, 24 February 1896, day of her profession."

Thérèse is twenty-three years old in these pictures, and she is soon to recognize the first symptoms of her fatal illness. She had completed the first section of her autobiography some two months before this photograph.

26A

26B

27

27. THÉRÈSE AND SISTER MARIE OF THE TRINITY BENEATH THE CROSS IN THE CLOISTER COURTYARD

Taken on the same day as the preceding photograph.

There exists in the Carmel's archives only a citrate proof fragment of a larger picture. The faces are rather blurred.

28A

28. THÉRÈSE AND SISTER MARTHE BENEATH THE CROSS IN THE CLOISTER COURTYARD

Taken on the same day. The 13 x 18 cm. glass negative is in poor condition. Thérèse's face is blurred.

Thérèse's figure was cut from this photograph, pasted on a picture of the cloister near the infirmary, and then re-photographed. This picture was never published, but it has been seen by some friends of the Carmel.

29

29. THÉRÈSE STANDING IN THE CLOISTER COURTYARD

This picture was taken, according to Céline's testimony, on March 17, 1896, the same day as the preceding photographs. The two sisters posed for similar pictures on that day, carrying almost the identical accessories.

The original 13 x 18 cm. plate has been lost, and there remained only a small citrate proof which shows Thérèse from the waist up and including the left hand. The inquiry we addressed to a number of religious communities in 1959–60 for a better copy of this proof produced the picture we present here, a photograph which offers every guarantee of authenticity.

At the Process for the Canonization, Céline testified: "After I had photographed the novices, I also took her portrait. She wanted to hold in her hand a scroll on which had been written the words of our holy Mother St. Teresa: 'I would give a thousand lives to save a single soul.'"

The 1955 Russian translation of *The Story of a Soul* uses this picture of Thérèse.

160

29A

29B

30A

30. FAMILY GROUP IN THE CHESTNUT WALK—1st POSE

Taken sometime after March 17, 1896, the investiture date of Marie Guérin, Thérèse's cousin, who is seen here in the novice's habit. There are no leaves yet on the chestnut trees, an indication that it was taken quite early in the spring. The 13 x 18 cm. glass negative is not an original, but one that was rephotographed from a proof mounted on a block of wood. The wooden mounting can be seen along the bottom of the photograph.

Marie Guérin is kneeling in front of the group; Pauline is seated on Thérèse's right; Céline is standing directly behind Thérèse, and Marie is on her right.

On the evening of April 2, Holy Thursday that year, Thérèse suffered her first lung hemorrhage. This photograph and the following one must have been taken sometime close to that date.

31A

31. FAMILY GROUP IN THE CHESTNUT WALK—2ND POSE

Taken on the same date and place as the preceding picture. The glass negative is also the same kind of secondary photograph as the preceding one.

The nuns have all turned their gaze in a different direction, and the faces are now rather tense.

166

32

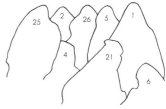

32. MOTHER MARIE DE GONZAGUE AND THE NOVITIATE GROUP

The original negative has been lost.

The photograph presented here is an oval citrate proof. The novices are gathered around Mother Gonzague on the profession day of Sister Marie of the Trinity, April 30, 1896.

32A

32B

33

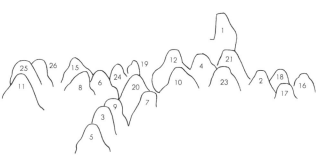

33A

33. THÉRÈSE EMBRACING THE CROSS IN THE CLOISTER COURTYARD: COMMUNITY GROUP—1ST POSE

Taken in July, 1896. The negative is glass, 13 x 18 cm.

Thérèse, standing on the concrete pedestal, is embracing the cross with both arms while presenting a lily to the figure of the Christ. Her face is rather blurred.

During this summer her physical condition is worsening, and she is also undergoing the violent temptations against faith which lasted until the time of her death.

34. THÉRÈSE EMBRACING THE CROSS IN THE CLOISTER COURTYARD: COMMUNITY GROUP—2ND POSE

Taken on the same occasion as the preceding picture. The glass negative, 13 x 18 cm., is misted at the bottom. Thérèse's face again is not completely in focus.

34A

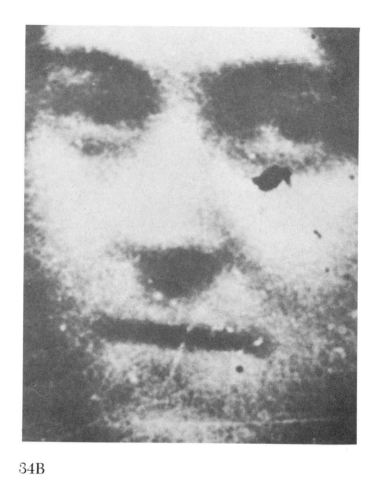

34B

35. THE COMMUNITY HAYING

Taken on the same day in July, 1896. The glass negative, 13 x 18 cm., is misted along the edges.

The community is haying in the meadow which stretches beside the chestnut walk. The walk can be seen at the right of the picture. As is customary when they do heavy work, the nuns have pinned up the outer fold of their habits. Sister St. John Baptist of the Sacred Heart (the second from the right) is holding in her hand the same lily Thérèse used in the two preceding photographs.

Thérèse moved, and her face is quite blurred. However, her picture is still very interesting, particularly the vigorous manner in which she is holding the pitchfork.

36. COMMUNITY GROUP BEFORE THE STATUE OF THE IMMACULATE HEART OF MARY

Taken in July, 1896. The negative is glass, 13 x 18 cm.

The community is arranged before the statue of the Immaculate Heart of Mary, which is in the rear garden of the Carmel. Thérèse's eyelids are partly closed, undoubtedly because the light is hurting her eyes.

36B

37

37. THÉRÈSE HOLDING A ROSARY

Taken in July, 1896, according to a written statement by Céline. Thérèse had already been sick for several months. The negative is glass, 13 x 18 cm., but the edges have been cropped to reduce its width.

The picture was taken by Céline in the courtyard outside the sacristy. But she was dissatisfied with the pose, as she wrote in her notes: "Her character was strong and virile, but now she ap-

peared timorous and fearful, and I was very much dissatisfied."

On the ground in front of Thérèse lies the lily she will hold in the following photograph.

This photograph was used as a frontispiece for some copies of the original 1898 edition of *The Story of a Soul;* the picture, however, was reversed for that publication.

37A

37B

38. THÉRÈSE HOLDING A LILY

Taken immediately after the preceding photograph. The negative is glass, 13 x 18 cm., but there are streaks in it which become more noticeable in the enlargements.

The picture was taken in the same sacristy courtyard, but the cross has been moved and Thérèse has shifted a little to her left, away from the corner of the wall.

"I made her straighten up," Céline writes, "and I asked her to face the camera and put on the expression she had in the picture the photographer took of the two of us when she was eight. After she complied with my instructions, I snapped the picture, without paying any attention to the arrangement of her habit. I was satisfied with this picture, as far as one can be satisfied with a photograph."

Thérèse did indeed comply with Céline's instructions, but her smile became tight and rigid during the long pose. She holds the lily awkwardly, as if she is somewhat embarrassed by this tribute. Mother Agnes wanted to destroy this picture because of the pose and the arrangement of the clothing, and she scratched the word "failure" across the gelatine of the negative. However, the face is so charming that this picture was used to illustrate the photostat edition of the autobiographical manuscripts released in 1956.

38A

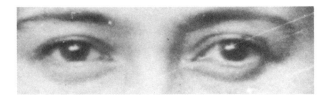

38B

38C

39. THÉRÈSE AS SACRISTAN, WITH HER SISTERS AND COUSIN— 1ST POSE

Taken in November, 1896. The negative is glass, 13 x 18 cm., but the gelatine along the right edge has curled back from the frame. The photograph was taken in the sacristy courtyard, which was the scene of a number of the preceding pictures. In comparing this with the Joan of Arc pictures (nos. 13 and 14), we can see the same section of wall, the same hook; but ivy has grown along the wall in the last year and a half. The picture was taken from a higher angle, but it was poorly focused since both Marie and Thérèse are partly excluded from the picture.

Thérèse held the office of sacristan until June, 1892, but she was reappointed for a short time after the community elections of March 21, 1896. This photograph and the following one were taken in November, 1896, some eleven months before her death. In September, shortly before this photograph, Thérèse had composed her letter to Marie, an explanation of her religious thought which forms the second section of the autobiography.

Marie Guérin is kneeling in front of the group. The Martin sisters are, from left to right: Marie, Pauline, Céline, and Thérèse.

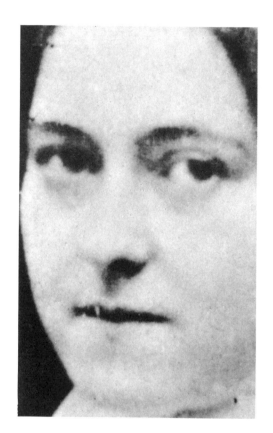

39B

40. THÉRÈSE AS SACRISTAN, WITH HER SISTERS AND COUSIN— 2ND POSE

A glass negative, 13 x 18 cm., taken on the same occasion.

Thérèse's face has been intentionally scratched over by her sisters. Léonie, her other sister at the Visitation Convent, furnishes an explanation in some lines she addressed to the Carmel on the back of a proof of this picture: "We like this group picture very much, and would like to have it in our archives. All of you took a good picture, except our Saint who leaves much to be desired. I would like you to retouch her, my dear artist, before returning

this charming tableau to us. Thank you!"

This photograph, and the preceding one, served as an inspiration for Céline's charcoal drawing "Sister Thérèse as Sacristan," which was used to illustrate editions of *The Story of a Soul* after 1912.

Picture 40 A is not an enlargement from the glass negative, but an original citrate proof which shows Thérèse before the negative was scratched. It is, however, somewhat grained and not as clear as the original negative.

40A

41. THÉRÈSE WITH THE HOLY PICTURES—1st POSE

The date of this picture, June 7, 1897, is written on the back of the photograph. The original negative has been lost, and the picture presented here is a film negative taken of a proof of the original.

The setting is again the sacristy courtyard. The two pictures Thérèse is holding are the Holy Face of Tours and the Infant Jesus, pictures which she kept in her breviary and which in some way summarize her spirituality.

On June 3, a few days earlier, Thérèse had started the final section of her autobiography. Since Thérèse's early death was now beyond doubt, her sisters wanted this photograph, and the two following ones, as a final remembrance of her appearance. The pictures were given to Mother Gonzague for her feast day, June 21. On July 8, Thérèse was moved into the infirmary where she spent the last two and a half months of her life.

41A

41B

42. THÉRÈSE WITH THE HOLY PICTURES—2ND POSE

A glass negative, 13 x 18 cm., taken on the same occasion.

Céline felt that Thérèse looked rather sad in the preceding picture. Thérèse is smiling faintly here, but the picture is blurred. The pose lasted nine seconds, and she had.a high fever.

Céline developed the negative immediately in a nearby cellar area. She was still unsatisfied with the result, and decided on a third pose. The word "failure" has been traced with a pin on the gelatine at the top of the negative.

42A

42B

43

43. THÉRÈSE WITH THE HOLY PICTURES—3RD POSE

Same occasion as the preceding. The negative is glass, 13 x 18 cm., but a shield has been used on the camera to limit the size of the picture.

Thérèse's mantle and veil are arranged differently, which indicates she changed position between poses. Everything is much more studied in this picture, and Thérèse seems to have employed a tremendous amount of effort to hold herself erect. She was so weak that a gardener who was working nearby heard her exclaim: "Oh quickly, I am exhausted!"

In a letter addressed to Abbé Bellière, Thérèse wrote of this photograph: "When the novices saw me they cried that I had taken on my grand look; it seems I am usually more smiling." However Thérèse herself liked the picture because she felt she appeared to be less fatigued.

This third pose was used in some copies of the original 1898 edition of *The Story of a Soul;* the picture, however, was reversed for that publication.

43A

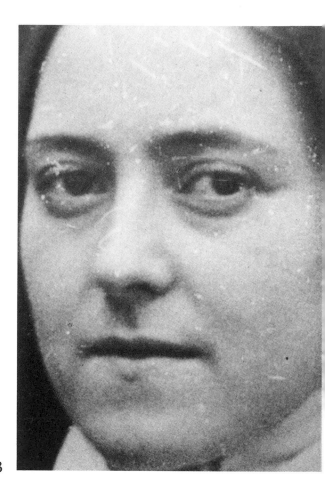

43B

44

44. THE NOVITIATE GROUP NEAR THE CROSS IN THE CLOISTER COURTYARD

Taken sometime after June 3, 1897, because Sister Marie of the Eucharist is wearing the black veil, and before July 8, the date Thérèse entered the infirmary. Perhaps it was taken the same date as the three preceding pictures in order to utilize the fourth plate contained in Céline's two photographic carriers; however that could be doubted, since Thérèse was severely exhausted on June 7. The negative is glass, 13 x 18 cm.; it is misted and not clearly focused. Thérèse's face is quite blurred.

Thérèse and her novices are shown casting flowers at the stone crucifix, but the prolonged pose made the nuns look stiff and artificial. Thérèse is holding the roses on her scapular; her eyes are closed.

209

44A

45

45. THÉRÈSE LYING ILL IN THE CLOISTER

Taken August 30, 1897. This is the last photograph of the Saint, taken exactly one month before her death. She is arranged in the cloister walk on a long reclining chair. The infirmary door is a few feet away, and a statue of St. Teresa of Avila can be dimly seen on the right.

Thérèse is wearing a simple night veil on her head, and over that a cap of white wool. The two straps of the small night scapular can be seen around her neck. Illness has made her face almost unrecognizable.

This photograph was first published in the *Novissima Verba* of 1923, but a black veil was painted over the white cap.

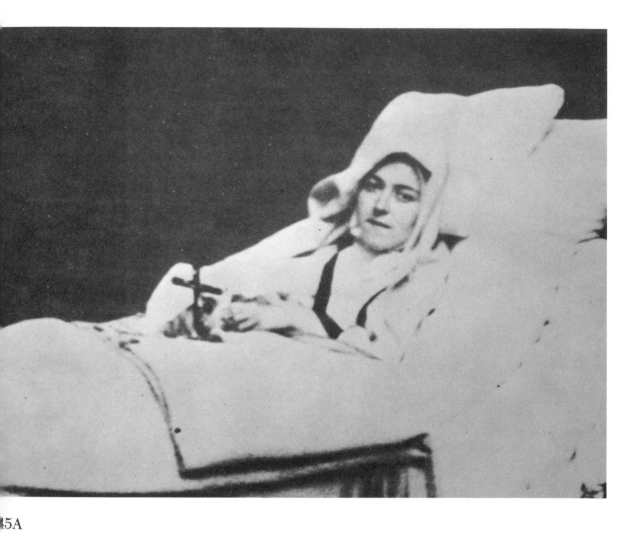

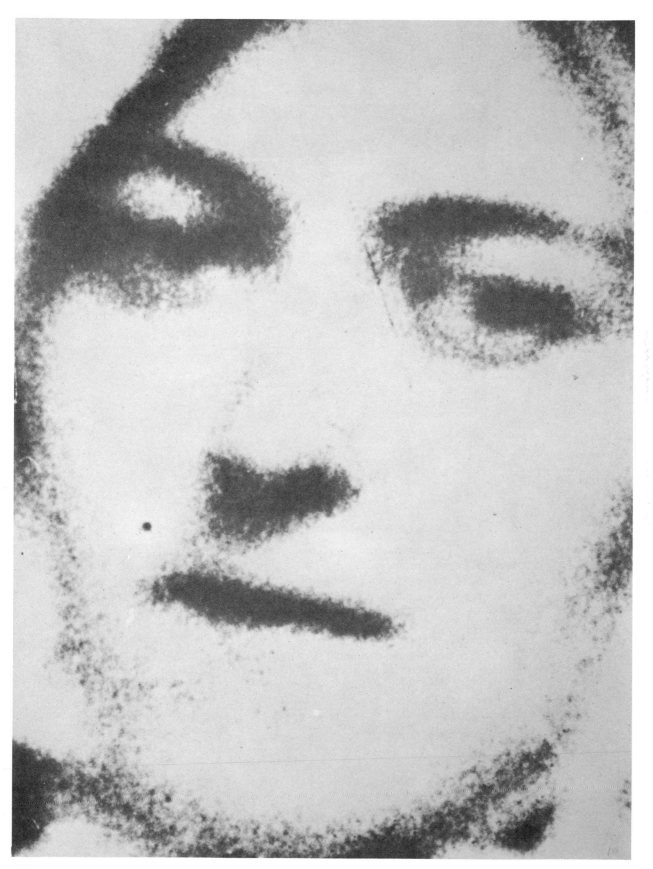

45B

46

46. THÉRÈSE IN DEATH—IN THE INFIRMARY

The original negative has been destroyed. In her memoirs, Céline informs us that she took a photograph of Thérèse in the infirmary on October 1, 1897, before the removal of the body. Unfortunately, the camera was only equipped for pictures of longer focus, and Céline did not have much space in the small infirmary; thus the picture had to be taken from a high angle. Furthermore, Thérèse's face was not in natural light. While Céline admitted that the photograph captured her sister's "heavenly smile," she did not, on the whole, like it because of the irregular play of lights and shadows. She preferred Thérèse's expression in her own 1905 drawing based on this picture.

The inquiry we conducted in the press and through circular letters in 1959–60 produced six photographs which are quite evidently prints of the original October 1, 1897, negative. These pictures are of unequal value. In two of them, Thérèse's figure has

46A

been cut out and remounted on a re-touched background. The most complete picture is a citrate proof pasted on a black card, which it seems was given by the Carmel to a hospital nun who, in turn, kindly loaned it to us. This proof is used here for picture 46. 46 A and 46 B are taken from another proof in which Thérèse's features are a little clearer.

Although we might not be able to prove the authenticity of this picture with absolute certitude, it nevertheless belongs in this album because of the strange and radiant beauty of Thérèse's face. Céline declared: "Even photography itself retouched Thérèse's face." Proofs of this picture were preserved in the convent for a certain time and several of the nuns were particularly fond of it. But researches in the archives were in vain; everything of this picture must have been destroyed.

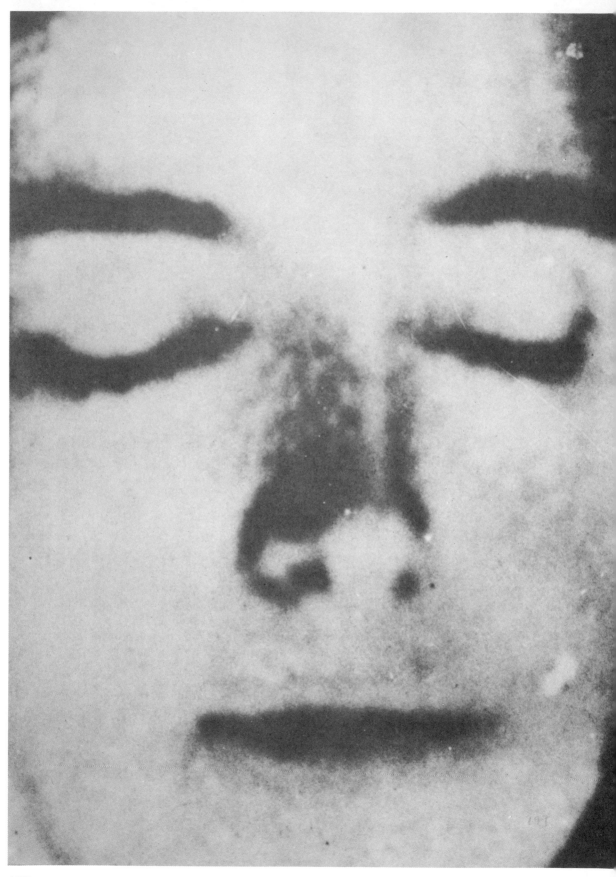

46B

47

47. THÉRÈSE IN DEATH—IN THE CHOIR

Taken four days after Thérèse's death, Sunday, October 3, 1897, while she was lying in her flower-covered coffin in the choir. In the background we can see the cloister door and the choir stall.

The Carmel considered this photograph a poor resemblance of Thérèse, and unfortunately the original negative was destroyed. We did discover, however, a contact proof of the negative which had been retouched with water colors, particularly around the eyes and the chin. The retouchings have been chemically removed through laboratory processes, and the present picture offers every guarantee of authenticity.

A slightly retouched version of this picture was used in the 1902 edition of *The Story of a Soul*. It was eliminated in the 1907 edition. The reason for its elimination is found in a statement by Mother Agnes: "We felt there was an air of majesty about her, but we did not recognize her any more."

218

47A

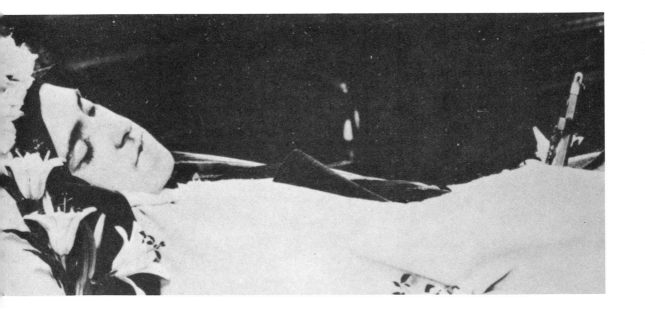

RESULTS OF THE INQUIRY CONDUCTED IN FRANCE AND ABROAD THROUGH THE PRESS AND BY CIRCULAR LETTERS ADDRESSED TO RELIGIOUS COMMUNITIES (1959–1960)

The inquiry brought: 384 pictures corresponding to those in album
108 pictures reproducing subjects already published by the Office Central de Lisieux
19 other imaginative pictures

These documents are here classified in the order of their importance:

NOS. OF THE PHOTOGRAPHS	SUBJECTS SHOWN	NO. OF REPLIES	CLASSIFICATION	
6	Thérèse as a novice without mantle	120	1st	
43	Thérèse with the holy pictures (3rd pose) June 7	84	2nd	
9	Group in the Lourdes courtyard (1st pose)	38	3rd	
20	Thérèse with her novices	28	4th	
39	Thérèse as sacristan (1st pose)	17	5th	equal in importance
47	Thérèse in death—in the choir	17	6th	
37	Thérèse holding a rosary	16	7th	
46	Thérèse in death—in the infirmary	12	8th	
45	Thérèse lying ill in the cloister	10	9th	
18	Community on the cloister porch	9	10th	equal in importance
3	Thérèse at thirteen	9	11th	
24	Community at the laundry (1st pose)	4	12th	equal in importance
29	Thérèse standing in the cloister courtyard	4	13th	
33	Thérèse embracing the cross in the cloister courtyard (1st pose)	3	14th	equal in importance
42	Thérèse with the holy pictures (2nd pose) June 7	3	15th	
2	Thérèse at eight with her sister Céline	2	16th	equal in importance
13	Thérèse as Joan of Arc in prison	2	17th	
14	Thérèse as Joan of Arc during her vision of St. Margaret	2	18th	
40	Thérèse as sacristan (2nd pose)	2	19th	
17	Community at recreation in chestnut walk (2nd pose)	1	20th	equal in importance
41	Thérèse with the holy pictures (1st pose) June 7	1	21st	

384

LIST OF NUNS APPEARING IN THE COMMUNITY GROUPS WITH ST. THÉRÈSE OF THE CHILD JESUS

1 Sister Thérèse of the Child Jesus (Sœur Thérèse de l'Enfant-Jésus et de la Sainte-Face), Thérèse Martin
2 Sister Marie of the Sacred Heart (Sœur Marie du Sacré-Cœur), Marie Martin
3 Reverend Mother Agnes of Jesus (Révérende Mère Agnès de Jésus), Pauline Martin
4 Sister Geneviève of the Holy Face (Sœur Geneviève de la Sainte-Face), Céline Martin
5 Sister Marie of the Eucharist (Sœur Marie de l'Eucharistie), Marie Guérin
6 Reverend Mother Marie de Gonzague

Other nuns in the order of their profession:

7 Sister St. Stanislas of the Sacred Hearts (Sœur Saint-Stanislas des Saints-Cœurs)
8 Mother Hermanda of the Heart of Jesus (Mère Hermance du Cœur de Jésus)
9 Sister Marie of the Angels and of the Sacred Heart (Sœur Marie des Anges et du Sacré Cœur)
10 Sister St. Raphael of the Heart of Mary (Sœur Saint-Raphael du Cœur de Marie)
11 Sister St. John the Baptist of the Heart of Jesus (Sœur Saint-Jean Baptiste du Cœur de Jésus)
12 Sister Amy of Jesus of the Heart of Mary (Sœur Aimée de Jésus et du Cœur de Marie)
13 Sister Teresa of Jesus of the Heart of Mary (Sœur Thérèse de Jésus du Cœur de Marie)
14 Sister Marguerite Marie of the Sacred Heart of Jesus (Sœur Marguerite-Marie du Sacré-Cœur de Jésus)
15 Sister Teresa of St. Augustine (Sœur Thérèse de Saint-Augustin)
16 Sister St. John of the Cross (Sœur Saint-Jean de la Croix)
17 Sister Marie Emmanuel (Sœur Marie-Emmanuel)
18 Sister Marie of St. Joseph (Sœur Marie de Saint-Joseph)
19 Sister Marie of Jesus (Sœur Marie de Jésus)
20 Sister Marie Philomena of Jesus (Sœur Marie-Philomène de Jésus)
21 Sister Marie of the Trinity (Sœur Marie de la Trinité)
22 Sister Anne of the Sacred Heart (Sœur Anne du Sacré-Cœur), of the Carmel in Saigon

Lay Sisters:

23 Sister Marie of the Incarnation (Sœur Marie de l'Incarnation)
24 Sister St. Vincent de Paul (Sœur Saint-Vincent de Paul)
25 Sister Marthe of Jesus (Sœur Marthe de Jésus)
26 Sister Mary Magdalene of the Blessed Sacrament (Sœur Marie-Madeleine
                                                    du Saint-Sacrement)

SUMMARY OF VARIOUS DOCUMENTS AND THEIR DEGREE OF AUTHENTICITY

FROM THE ORIGINAL GLASS NEGATIVES:
        2 - 4 - 5 - 6 - 7 - 8 - 9 - 11 - 12 - 13 - 14 - 16 - 17 - 18 - 19 -
        20 - 21 - 22 - 23 - 24 - 25 - 28 - 33 - 34 - 35 - 36 - 37 - 38 -
        39 - 40 - 42 - 43 - 44 - 45

PLATES MADE FROM PROOFS OF ORIGINALS:
        30 - 31 - 41

CITRATE-CONTACT PROOFS MADE FROM ORIGINALS:
        15 - 27 - 29 - 32

PHOTOGRAPHS FROM WHICH RETOUCHING HAS BEEN REMOVED:
        3 - 10 - 26 - 47

PHOTOGRAPHS OF INTEREST BUT FROM SECONDARY SOURCES:
        1 - 46

PLACES IN THE CONVENT WHERE THE VARIOUS PHOTOGRAPHS WERE TAKEN

The letters and figures below, showing the different locations in the convent and grounds, are taken from the architectural plan reproduced on the end sheets. They are followed by the number of the photographs taken in each of these places.

I^a	Statue of Our Lady of Lourdes	9 - 10 - 23
I	Lourdes courtyard	19 - 20
C	Sacristy courtyard	11 - 12 - 13 - 14 - 15? - 37 - 38 - 39 - 40 - 41 - 42 - 43
G	Choir	47
12	Statue of the Blessed Virgin (called of the Heart of Mary)	36
U	Infirmary of St. Teresa	46
Z^f	Statue of St. Teresa of Avila beside the infirmary door	45
Z^d	Cloister courtyard	18 - 29
Z^a	Cross in the cloister courtyard	5 - 6 - 21 - 22 - 26 - 27 - 28 - 33 - 34 - 44
9	Laundry	24 - 25
5	Chestnut walk	16 - 17 - 30 - 31 - 32
1	Infirmary courtyard	7 - 8
2	Meadow	35

PLAN OF CONVENT AND GROUND

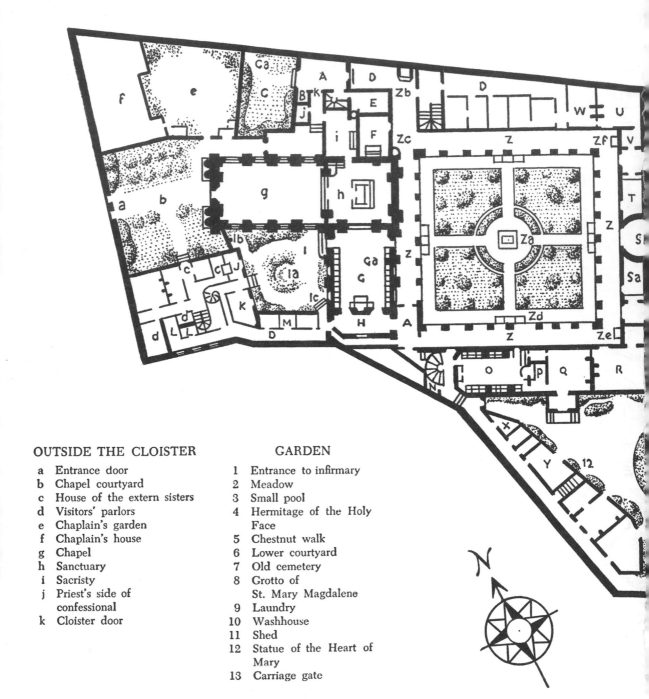

OUTSIDE THE CLOISTER

a Entrance door
b Chapel courtyard
c House of the extern sisters
d Visitors' parlors
e Chaplain's garden
f Chaplain's house
g Chapel
h Sanctuary
i Sacristy
j Priest's side of
   confessional
k Cloister door

GARDEN

1 Entrance to infirmary
2 Meadow
3 Small pool
4 Hermitage of the Holy
   Face
5 Chestnut walk
6 Lower courtyard
7 Old cemetery
8 Grotto of
   St. Mary Magdalene
9 Laundry
10 Washhouse
11 Shed
12 Statue of the Heart of
   Mary
13 Carriage gate